The
Parent's Guide
to
Birdnesting

A Child-Centered Solution
to Co-Parenting During
Separation and Divorce

Ann Gold Buscho, PhD

ADAMS MEDIA
New York London Toronto Sydney New Delhi

Adams Media
An Imprint of Simon & Schuster, Inc.
57 Littlefield Street
Avon, Massachusetts 02322

First Adams Media trade paperback edition September 2020

ADAMS MEDIA and colophon are trademarks of Simon & Schuster.

For information about special discounts for bulk purchases, please contact Simon & Schuster Special Sales at 1-866-506-1949 or business@simonandschuster.com.

The Simon & Schuster Speakers Bureau can bring authors to your live event. For more information or to book an event contact the Simon & Schuster Speakers Bureau at 1-866-248-3049 or visit our website at www.simonspeakers.com.

Interior design by Priscilla Yuen
Illustrations by Alaya Howard

Manufactured in the United States of America

10 9 8 7 6 5 4 3 2 1

Library of Congress Cataloging-in-Publication Data
Names: Gold Buscho, Ann, author.
Title: The parent's guide to birdnesting / Ann Gold Buscho, PhD.
Description: Avon, Massachusetts: Adams Media, 2020. | Includes bibliographical references and index.
Identifiers: LCCN 2020011313 | ISBN 9781507214091 (pb) | ISBN 9781507214107 (ebook)
Subjects: LCSH: Parenting, Part-time. | Children of divorced parents—Family relationships. | Single parents.
Classification: LCC HQ759.915 .G625 2020 | DDC 306.85/6—dc23
LC record available at https://lccn.loc.gov/2020011313

ISBN 978-1-5072-1409-1
ISBN 978-1-5072-1410-7 (ebook)

Dedication

To my sister, Judy Gold, who unfailingly believed in me and always encouraged me to write. I miss her every day.

Acknowledgments

I couldn't have written this book without my clients and several friends who shared their stories with me. The stories are all based on their real experiences, but names and details have been changed throughout the book to protect their confidentiality.

Thanks to my good friend and collaborative divorce colleague Judith F. Sterling, who advised me on everything related to finances in Chapter 4. The budget worksheets are all her creations.

Thanks to my dear friend, Irene, for the more than fifty years of friendship, for the many times she read my drafts, and for the many meals she cooked for me while I was sequestered in my writing room.

To my children, Sarah, Sasha, and David, for encouraging me to write, and for letting me neglect them (and their babies) while I was writing.

Thanks to my father, a writer himself, for his steadfast encouragement (and at times gentle nagging) and enthusiasm for my writing.

Thanks also to my husband, Joel, who has become a stellar editor. Without his emotional support and commitment to our marriage, I would not have had the courage or the strength to write this book.

Thanks also to my brilliant editors. Alan Rinzler helped me shape the book from a stodgy academic text to something people might want to read. Laura Daly, at Adams Media, helped me make the book publishable, and with delightful good nature and great patience.

Contents

Introduction

Going through a separation and/or divorce as a family is a challenging time filled with change and uncertainty. Figuring out how to best help children manage this transition is often parents' primary concern. Who will be with the children when? How will the children be brought from one place to another? One idea that can minimize some of the stress on children is to consider "nesting." Nesting, or "birdnesting," as it's sometimes known, refers to a transitional or temporary arrangement where the children stay in the family home and parents take turns living there and being "on duty" with their children. This plan gives children more time to adapt to changes in the family and means they don't have to immediately move. Like birds who alternately swoop in and out, caring for the babies while the babies remain safe and secure in their soft, protected nest, parents work together to create a home for their children that is safe, stable, and loving. Parents also use this time to consider the future of their marriage and decide to work on reconciliation or move toward separation or divorce.

The main goals of nesting arrangements are to stabilize your family during a difficult time and to provide a respite—for you and for your children—from conflict. No matter what decisions are ultimately made about your relationship, this period of time could have a strong impact on your children's lives—but it doesn't have to be an entirely negative one. Imagine that years from now your children will sit with friends and tell the story of their parents' relationship and divorce. What story do you want them to share? You and your spouse do have some control over how this stage looks and feels to your children. The decisions and actions happening now shape their future narratives. I believe that nesting can offer a better chance for your children to share a healthier and more harmonious narrative of the situation—or, at least, a less adversarial view of separation or divorce.

I am a psychologist with more than twenty-five years of experience working with children, parents, and families. But I also have firsthand experience with nesting. In 1993 my ex-husband and I set up a nesting agreement in order to keep our children in a stable environment while we made our decisions about the next steps. At that time, few had heard of nesting. Our marriage counselor suggested that we consider this arrangement, and once we discussed it, we agreed. We nested for fifteen months until our divorce was complete, we understood our finances, and we had decided what our future living arrangements would be. Our children (then six, ten, and fourteen) had adjusted to a schedule of shared parenting and were able to begin transitioning between two homes. Looking back, I believe that the nesting period helped all of us to move on and eased the turmoil of the separation and divorce.

In the years following my own experience, I learned the variety of options available in nesting arrangements and how each family needs to choose what works best for them. I learned how to set up agreements that meet the needs of the entire family. As an advocate of providing a nesting period for divorcing families, I developed a more detailed and structured approach that helps prevent some of the potential obstacles, some of which my ex and I experienced.

I've helped many different types of families manage this period of adjustment with as much thoughtfulness, grace, and respect as possible. A successful nesting experience truly has the power to preserve and even strengthen your relationship with your children by giving them a stable and secure home during this time of transition. Let nesting help your family transition from one phase of life to another with the peace and harmony you all deserve.

Part One

Getting Started

IN THE FIRST PART OF THIS BOOK, you will learn about the basics of nesting and its benefits, for you and your partner *and* your children. You will explore the factors that could make nesting a great option for you, as well as the logistics of setting up your successful nesting living arrangements. Some issues can make nesting difficult, and we will consider those as well. As you understand the goals of nesting and the process of transitioning into a nesting arrangement, you will be able to decide if nesting would be right for your family.

Along the way, in the Case in Point sections, you will meet several families who considered and chose various nesting options based on what worked for their circumstances. Their stories and insights will provide real-life examples of how nesting can work. If you decide it's right for you, you'll find step-by-step instructions for creating a successful nesting plan, including drafting a complete parenting plan to support your co-parenting arrangement.

CHAPTER 1

What Is Nesting?

While you and your partner work through the future of your relationship, nesting can provide structure and stability for your children as you co-parent. In this chapter, you will learn what nesting can look like in real life, how the on-duty and off-duty parenting system works, and about various potential living arrangements. Understanding the goals and benefits of nesting for yourself and for your children will help you make an informed choice about whether it's right for your family.

Nesting, Explained

Nesting is an arrangement where the children stay in the family home, and the parents rotate in and out for their scheduled parenting time. The term comes from a comparison with bird nests, where the babies stay in the nests and the parents come in and out of it, caring for the babies. Nesting looks different for every family, and the most successful nesting arrangements are carefully personalized.

Nesting parents work out clear and written agreements about communication, schedules, parenting, and finances, tailored to their situation. What every nesting arrangement has in common is the goal of reducing conflict and providing a consistent, stable home for the children while the marital status is in flux. In some cases, nesting is used as a transition between marriage and divorce, and in other cases, it is used as a temporary separation while partners work through marital or personal problems. Some people call themselves "apartners" since they are parenting together but aren't romantically involved.

A stable schedule is one of the cornerstones of nesting. You and your spouse would alternate being in the home with your children on an agreed-upon schedule that is clear, ideally in writing. The on-duty parent stays in the home with your children, and the off-duty parent is usually in another location. It's crucial to create a predictable schedule for your children that helps them feel secure, although some flexibility in the schedule is also important. For example, the schedule may include some flexibility to allow each parent to meet their work schedules, but overall the system should be as consistent as possible. When you schedule this on- and off-duty time so carefully, you will have time to adjust to being a single parent, and everyone (including your children) knows who is on duty.

WHAT DOES THE ON-DUTY PARENT DO?

When you are the on-duty parent, you will care for your children. That includes getting your children up in the morning, getting them to school, picking them up if they need that, making sure they get to their extracurricular activities or doctor's appointments, helping them with their homework, if any, and making sure they have a good dinner and get to bed on time. When parents are nesting, the on-duty parent is also responsible for the house, laundry, and repairs, or if the pantry needs to be restocked.

WHAT DOES THE OFF-DUTY PARENT DO?

When the on-duty parent turns over the responsibility of the children to the other parent according to the schedule you have created, he or she goes off duty. The off-duty parent leaves all parenting to the on-duty parent and normally doesn't come into the home or the child's life without prior agreement. (For example, you can decide whether the off-duty parent would be welcome at a family event or an extracurricular activity, say a soccer game or school play.)

FINDING ADDITIONAL HELP

The off-duty parent is freed from parental duties unless agreed to otherwise. For example, if the on-duty parent is unavailable during any point of her or his on-duty time, that parent might give the off-duty parent an option to step in. If the off-duty parent isn't available, the on-duty parent is responsible for finding alternate care.

WHERE DOES THE OFF-DUTY PARENT LIVE?

There are many options for parents' personal living arrangements when they are not staying in the family home. When they are off duty, parents can live in the following:

- Separate areas within the home (e.g., an in-law apartment and a bedroom)
- An off-site residence they share (e.g., the off-duty parent always uses it)

- Separate apartments or houses
- Homes of friends or family

Obviously, many factors will play into determining which living situation works best for your family. We'll talk more about this topic in Chapter 2.

WHO SHOULD TRY NESTING?

Nesting works best for parents who are equally involved in parenting, who see parents as equally important in child-rearing, and who have some understanding of child development and the effect of divorce on children. In addition, nesting ordinarily appeals more to parents who have the financial means to support separate living arrangements. Nesting also works well for parents who are generally able to communicate respectfully with each other and who can commit to leaving the family home in a reasonable condition when turning over the duties to the other parent.

Nesting is not for everyone. You will have to consider whether you and your spouse each feel emotionally able to continue to share a home while taking a break or moving toward a long-term separation. You have to trust each other enough to be able to speak openly about your expectations and concerns. You'll need a well-thought-out plan that will work for both of you and your kids. This book will show you how to accomplish all of these things.

RELIGIOUS AND CULTURAL CONSIDERATIONS

Divorce and nesting among mainstream Americans fit with cultural ideals of freedom, individualism, the pursuit of happiness, and self-actualization. In contrast to mainstream American culture, almost all orthodox religions discourage or forbid divorce, and families following these religions would not be likely candidates for nesting.

Less conservative religious people, however, often find a way to preserve some of their traditional values while considering more modern ideas like nesting. Your and your partner's cultural background might also play a role in whether or not nesting would be an option.

What Does Nesting Look Like in Real Life?

No matter your living situation and work schedule, with some creative, out-of-the-box thinking, you can develop a successful living arrangement if you decide to nest. Here are some examples of how different families made it work.

- My ex and I alternated weeks with the children, and in my off-duty time, I rented a room in a house with four other renters. My ex stayed with friends during most of his off-duty time, although he did rent a small cottage near the family home. The weekly rotation was not ideal for our younger children (who typically need more frequent contact with both parents) but necessary to accommodate our work schedules, and we agreed to midweek dinners when the children ate with the off-duty parent.

- One couple I worked with were able to divide the rooms in their home, designating specific rooms for both the on- and off-duty parent. It was helpful for them to save money, and because their children were very young, they decided to alternate their on-duty time every three days. While their home was big enough to do this, they had some challenges around boundaries: Access to the kitchen was the major one. The other challenge for them was that the children often sought contact with the off-duty parent who was elsewhere in the home. Fortunately, they were able to make their nesting arrangement work after a few weeks of experimenting with different solutions.

- Another family I counseled lived in a small rented apartment and wanted to find a way to nest. They couldn't afford to pay rent elsewhere, but they were able to stay with friends and relatives nearby. They agreed to a schedule of rotating into the home roughly every four days. They continued to nest until their legal process was finished.

- Another family was able to convert their basement to make it more comfortable, and both parents used it when off duty. Because this area had a separate entrance, each parent had the privacy he needed when off duty.

CASE IN POINT

I had been working with Jack and Allie for eight months when Jack announced that he wanted a divorce. When I raised the possibility of nesting to give them some time to consider their next steps, Allie said, "I'm not sure I could do that. I'm so angry about all of this—how will nesting help me settle down? And how are we supposed to co-parent together when we can hardly talk to each other without it becoming an argument?"

I addressed her concerns about arguments and talked about how hard it had been for their children to see their parents' frequent fighting. They agreed that they were both worn out from the conflict and could use a time-out. I explained that nesting could ease the stress for them and their children, so Jack and Allie agreed to think about it. They needed some time to consider whether they could set aside their emotions for the sake of the children. When they returned the following week, they were ready to talk about a nesting arrangement that would work for them.

The Goals of Nesting

Each couple has their own reasons to try nesting, but here are some common goals:

- **To offer a solid structure to your family life despite the parents' separation.** When you are considering separation or divorce, you may feel that your world is turning upside down. It is an overwhelming period, as you try to sort through both the emotional side of the situation (your many feelings) and the logistical one (the process of whether or how the family will transition to a new structure). Nesting can nail down some key parts of your life as you navigate the future.

- **To provide safety and stability for your children.** In all my years of private practice, I have yet to meet parents who did not want to provide security, structure, and predictability for their children during difficult times. You and your spouse may have poor communication patterns, different parenting styles, conflicts, or different goals in life. Perhaps you have difficulties in decision-making or feel you simply no longer love your spouse. Whatever the state of your marriage, and even if you don't agree on many things, you probably agree that you want your kids to be safe, happy, and thrive.

- **To end the marital strife.** Nesting gives you and your spouse some respite from the tension or conflict in the marriage so that you can think through your decisions. You may be worn out by the difficulties that led to your decision to separate. Nesting might help ease ongoing strain so that you feel more able to make difficult choices and move forward.

The Benefits of Nesting

Nesting arrangements do take time and effort to work out, but they're well worth your energy. Here are some of the benefits your family can experience:

- **Nesting can support the creation or continuation of your children's positive and secure attachment to each of you.** In my work with families, I see the importance of children having a secure attachment to each parent, despite their parents' marriage ending. According to the research of John Bowlby and his colleague Mary Ainsworth, a secure attachment to each parent may predict future healthy relationships, build your children's self-esteem and resilience, and allow your kids to adjust and adapt to a new family structure. Facilitating these important attachments is easier with nesting. For example, the parent who has had less parenting time during the marriage (often the breadwinner and stereotypically the dad) now can develop closer ties with the children while "coming up to speed" as a solo parent.

- **Nesting will help you adjust to being a single parent.** Successful nesting will give you and your co-parent time to be fully involved in your children's growth and upbringing.

- **You'll know what your children will experience in the future if you plan to have them move from one place to another as you co-parent them.** If or when you move to separate homes, you will have gained empathy for your children's experience of moving from one home to the other.

- **Nesting gives you time and space to deal with your emotions.** "Don't make big decisions in a crisis" is my mantra. In a crisis (such as a separation), you just need to get through one day at a time while you take care of yourself and your children. It's said that divorce is 95 percent emotional and only 5 percent legal. The legal process requires major decisions about things that will affect you for the rest of your life. Unfortunately, many people initiate their legal divorce process at a time when they are in no condition to make big decisions about anything. You're mistaken if you believe that initiating the divorce, or racing through it, will make you feel better. Take the time to deal with the emotional part first. Nesting gives you that opportunity because it gives you respite from the marital stress with little disruption to your children. Counseling could also help you get back on your feet. I think that most divorces would go much more easily if people waited until their emotions were more settled before starting a legal process. (See Chapter 8 for more on processing your emotions.)

- **Successful nesting will ease your children's stress in the short term.** For some children, it is a great relief when the arguments stop. In my experience, children can adjust and adapt to a new family structure within a year or two, provided their parents cocreate a safe, nurturing home, free from excessive conflict. Minimizing parental conflict during and after the divorce is the single most important thing you can do to support the well-being and success of your children in the long term. Research showing the potentially harmful effects of couple or interparental conflict on children has been well documented since the 1930s.

CASE IN POINT

Cathy was the daughter of immigrant Chinese parents. When she married her Caucasian husband, it took time for her family to accept him. Like many first-generation immigrants, Cathy had internalized her parents' traditional values and beliefs while assimilating American ideas.

Later, when her husband pursued a divorce, Cathy's parents blamed her for the breakup. Cathy also blamed herself. As in many community-centered or "collectivist" cultures, she and her family believed that it is always the wife's responsibility to hold the marriage and family together. Traditionally, self-sacrifice, silent suffering, and perseverance are held up as valued virtues for Asian women, especially in marriage.

Cathy was tormented by shame and continued to blame herself for the breakup. The shame made it hard for her to imagine sharing the home and developing a co-parenting relationship with her soon-to-be ex. Over several weeks, she began to process her emotions and was then able to understand the benefits of nesting for their children.

KEY POINTS TO REMEMBER

- Nesting is an arrangement where the children stay in the family home, and the parents alternate or rotate into the home for their scheduled on-duty parenting time.

- When off duty, parents might live in a specific area of the family home, stay outside the home (with friends or relatives, or in a rented studio or other location).

- Nesting looks different for every family. Successful nesting arrangements are designed specifically for the needs and comfort of your family.

- The goal of nesting is to reduce conflict and provide a consistent, stable home for the children while the marital status is in flux. Minimizing parental conflict during and after the divorce is the single most important thing you can do to support the well-being and success of your children in the long term.

- Nesting will give you time to make decisions about the future of your marriage and the space to chart a path toward divorce or reconciliation.

- Nesting will continue as long as it is working for all of you, and it will end when you or your spouse decide to move to separate homes or to reconcile.

- Successful nesting requires clear, written agreements about communication, schedules, parenting, and finances, tailored to your unique situation.

CHAPTER 2

Is Nesting Right for Your Family?

You may be asking yourself these questions:

- How can I be sure nesting is right for our family's circumstances?

- What if we aren't sure about the future of our relationship and need some emotional space to think things through?

- How can we live and parent under the same roof when we have decided to separate or divorce but can't afford to move to separate homes?

- How can we give our children time to adjust to one family under two roofs?

In this chapter, we'll look closely at the factors to consider in making your decision to nest. We'll look at the pros and cons of nesting, and most importantly, we'll help you determine whether nesting is the right choice for you and your family.

Assessing Your Ability to Co-Parent Questionnaire

This quiz is designed to help you and your partner think about key areas of your lives and identify potentially problematic areas. Your answers may help you decide whether nesting is a good fit for your current partnership.

If a statement is generally true, mark T, and if generally false, mark F. Each parent should answer separately and as honestly as you can. You can do this questionnaire alone or with a therapist or counselor if you have one.

		True	False
1.	I am able to ask for help or support and am willing to accept it.		
2.	My partner is able to ask for help or support and is willing to accept it.		
3.	We are good problem-solvers when it comes to our kids.		
4.	I feel my partner listens well and understands me.		
5.	I think I am a good listener.		
6.	I know the kids are in good hands with my partner.		
7.	I believe my partner knows the kids are in good hands with me.		
8.	We work well together when it comes to parenting.		
9.	I know when to take a time-out.		

	True	False
10. My partner knows when to call for a time-out.		
11. We argue more often when I have been drinking.		
12. We argue more often when my partner has been drinking.		
13. It is important to me that both of us parent our children.		
14. I don't think my partner values my point of view.		
15. My partner doesn't think I value his or her point of view.		
16. I am afraid of my partner's reactions.		
17. I have threatened, pushed, shoved, grabbed, or slapped my partner.		
18. My partner has threatened, pushed, shoved, grabbed, or slapped me.		
19. We can make decisions together and keep our agreements.		
20. I think we cooperate pretty well with each other.		
21. When it comes to raising our children, my partner's opinion matters to me.		
22. I think communication is a large problem for us.		
23. Good communication is important to me.		
24. My partner has a lot to offer our children.		

	True	False
25. I worry about my partner's use of drugs or alcohol.		
26. My partner has expressed concern about my use of drugs or alcohol.		
27. I don't respect my partner's parenting style.		
28. My partner criticizes my parenting style.		
29. We have mostly the same values when it comes to our kids.		
30. I keep my promises and agreements.		
31. My partner keeps his or her promises and agreements.		
32. I go along just to get along because I don't like fighting.		
33. My partner is inappropriate with our children.		
34. I worry about my kids when they are with my partner.		

After you finish, note and appreciate together the statements where you are in agreement. Then discuss the ones where your responses do not agree.

Now look for any "red flags" you or your spouse may have noted. Red flag items are 11, 12, 16, 17, 18, 25, 26, 27, 28, 33, and 34. If either you or your spouse has marked any of these questions as "true," it is important to discuss them carefully, probably with a therapist or counselor. These are questions that may indicate that nesting is not right for your family, or that it will fail unless you address those concerns before you begin the nesting.

After comparing and discussing these questions with your spouse, you'll notice that in addition to good-enough communication, respect, trust, and safety are important in co-parenting and in nesting. These qualities can be cultivated in your nesting situation if both you and your spouse are committed to doing that. The discussion of your responses and the outcome of your discussions will help you decide whether nesting might work well for you.

CASE IN POINT

When Jack and Allie came back the next week to talk about nesting, we discussed their responses to the questionnaire. They were anxious to discuss the questions where they were not in agreement. Since none of the red flag issues were present, I suggested that nesting was an option they could consider in order to give each of them some relief from the frequent and painful arguments. I assured them that couples rarely agree on all of the statements in the questionnaire and that those differences could indicate where they could try to improve their co-parenting relationship.

"But I don't want to ruin the kids' lives if we decide to separate," Allie said. "I'm worried that their lives will be turned upside down."

"With your kids in a secure and stable home," I told them, "you won't have to worry so much about disrupting their lives. You can ensure their stability and support them while you're figuring out what you want to do about your marriage. Their routines may not change much while nesting, and they'd have quality time with each of you."

I asked them to think about whether they were willing to put their children's welfare ahead of their own. Allie said she was willing to do that but worried that the kids would still be upset later if the situation changed and the kids *did* have to rotate from one parent's home to the other's.

I explained, "Nesting parents experience firsthand what their children may experience when they later live under their parents' two roofs. You'll be more empathetic and aware of potential obstacles. Still, keeping your children's lives as undisturbed as possible now, while you two sort through your issues, can help prevent long-term emotional damage to your kids."

Issues to Consider Before Nesting

The questionnaire you just finished touches on a wide variety of factors that can indicate whether or not nesting might work for you and your family. This section will dive deeper into some of the more important issues that you should talk through with your spouse before proceeding.

CAN YOU WORK AROUND POTENTIAL PITFALLS?

If you know of areas that could present challenges to nesting, are you two well equipped to handle them? For example, one parent may be caring for his or her own aging parent, or have a demanding work schedule. If you can anticipate potential pitfalls, you might be able to overcome them and nest.

CAN YOU PRACTICE "GOOD-ENOUGH COMMUNICATION"?

In many situations when a couple is separating, communication breaks down in one way or another. If that's the case with you and your partner, it's unrealistic to think your communication will suddenly become stellar as you nest, but that's all right. Keep your expectations reasonable and aim for *good-enough communication*. Good-enough communication conveys information or requests without venting your emotional reactions. It is pragmatic; it means that you and your co-parent can communicate effectively about logistics, such as changes in the schedule, something going on with a child, or matters of finance or home maintenance. The communication is "good enough" to get the job done.

Good-enough communication means that you can ask for a change or describe an issue calmly, objectively, and succinctly. Communication may not be "perfect" all the time, but if you can focus on good-enough communication most of the time, your children will benefit from it and feel well cared for by both parents. Here's an example of good-enough communication: "Jake failed his spelling test last week. Let's both spend a little more time drilling him for his test this Friday." The statement is neutral and non-blaming. Another example: "Something has come up at work, and I won't be able to collect the kids tonight. Are you able to keep them overnight, and I will get them in the morning to take them to school?"

Even if communication, flexibility, and trust are exactly the things that went wrong in your relationship, you still might be able to practice good-enough communication. The question is whether you can set aside your own feelings for the sake of your children. When your own emotions are in flux, as they typically are during a marital crisis, it can be both challenging and stressful to work cooperatively and to tailor a plan. However, in my practice, I've seen that many parents can set aside their emotions when they focus on their children's welfare. If you aren't sure how to get started, it may help if you bring in a neutral facilitator, such as a mental health professional who specializes in divorce-related issues.

CASE IN POINT

The key to avoiding so many pitfalls in nesting is good-enough communication. I watched a nesting arrangement almost unravel when a father named Derek hired a babysitter to care for their children, rather than offering that opportunity to his available, but off-duty spouse, Deb. Deb asked, "How can we make this work if he won't let me take the kids when he's not home?" She was so angry that she threatened to end the nesting, but they were able to revisit their agreements and commit to offering time to the off-duty parent before bringing in alternate care.

Upsets such as these tend to be predictable. This book will help you spot situations like this ahead of time so you can work out how you want to handle them before they happen. If a snafu still occurs, though, instead of feeling sad or angry about it, try to see it as a learning opportunity to help you practice good-enough communication and refine your agreements.

CAN YOU SET UP A WORKABLE SCHEDULE?

Scheduling is a cornerstone of nesting, but it's also an area filled with complexity, variables, and unexpected changes. Your family is probably juggling several schedules at one time:

1. **Each parent's work schedule:** Talk through questions like this: If one or both of you work outside the home, how will your children be cared for when they're not in school or don't even go to school yet?

2. **Each of your children's current schedule:** What are your children's schedules during the school year and during school breaks? Who takes them to school and picks them up? What after-school activities are they involved with, and how will their pickups and drop-offs be handled while nesting?

The key is to find a nesting arrangement that allows those schedules to be met in addition to the following:

• **Minimizing disruption:** A successful nesting schedule provides as little disruption to your children's schedule as possible. For example, if one of you works full time outside the home, the other might care for your children after school until the on-duty parent comes home from work. In a family with two working parents, perhaps the same childcare provider, daycare, or family member who has been caring for your children before you've been nesting can continue to do so, regardless of which parent is on or off duty.

• **Maximizing your children's time with each of you:** The most successful nesting agreements maximize the time the children have with each parent. Not only is that usually best for the children, but it also feels respectful to the other parent. Nesting works best if parents can divide their time with the children more or less equally. If one of you is only available on the weekends, for example, or on an unpredictable basis due to work, travel, or other constraints, nesting is not impossible, but it will be challenging. In these situations, the parent who is with the children most of the time would need to find short-term alternate housing when the less available parent can be on duty. This might be staying with friends or relatives, or renting an Airbnb.

CASE IN POINT

Angela had been a full-time mom since their children, now eight and thirteen, were born. Her husband, Don, had a management position in a rapidly growing Internet company and frequently had to work late, attend off-site meetings with short notice, and train new employees in offices throughout the country. Once they decided to separate, Don's intention was to "do fifty-fifty," but after thinking it through, he realized to be a single parent he would have to significantly change his career path, which was not what he wanted to do.

In a situation such as this, it made more sense to set up a schedule that worked with Don's work schedule and maximized his time with their children. Don had to adjust his schedule so that he was able to be home one week every month. "This is the best I can do," he said, "if I want to continue to get promotions." Angela agreed that his income benefited the family, and so she agreed to the arrangement. Angela stayed with a friend when off duty, and nesting ultimately worked out well for them and for their children.

ARE BOTH OF YOU EMOTIONALLY ABLE TO HANDLE THIS CHANGE?

Think about how it will feel for you to move in and out of your family home at a time when so much of your future seems uncertain. This is a big adjustment for most parents. It is probably painful to leave your children, and your off-duty living situation may not be as comfortable or familiar as your home. One father told me, "Every time I have to leave the house, I just get all pissed off again. I just want to be in my own place all the time." Leaving at the end of your on-duty time triggers a lot of feelings: grief and guilt being the most common. Over time, these emotions will likely ease, and the transitions in and out of the home feel less upsetting.

Try to see any silver lining to the situation that can help you manage your emotions. For example, you may be looking forward to some time alone or to activities that you set aside while on duty. One parent had taken up painting as a way to express her feelings, and she looked forward to time in her studio. When I nested, I was able to schedule most of my patient workload for my off-duty time. This was a welcome distraction from the sadness I felt leaving my children and home. (We'll talk more in Part 3 about how you can take care of yourself and your emotions during the time you are nesting; for now, just think about feelings you might have.)

One issue to be careful of is the temptation to do too much together. For example, Jack and Allie scheduled a weekly Sunday night dinner for the entire family. In the beginning, the on-duty parent cooked and invited the off-duty parent to dinner. Later, they began to meet at their favorite diner. Their hope was to reassure the children that their parents could still be together and co-parent without arguing. At some point, this arrangement became confusing for their children. When I met with the children separately, their daughter Sophie asked me about it. "We love Sunday dinners all together, but if they get along so well on Sundays, why are they getting divorced?"

Sometimes, even parents who like the idea of nesting conclude that it would not make sense for their family. This might be because the parents have different views of the future of the marriage. That is, one parent wants to nest in order to stay connected in some way to the other parent, hoping to have more contact and the partner will change her or his mind about the divorce. Another parent might find it too painful to even see the partner's personal possessions in the home. Another example is when one parent has already started a new relationship and wants a more complete separation from the spouse. The bottom line is that nesting does require a certain amount of emotional stability, so you should think about whether you and your partner have that.

IS NESTING THE BEST CHOICE FOR YOUR KIDS?

You and your spouse know your kids best and will need to talk about what nesting arrangement would work well for them. Here are some factors to consider:

1. **Their age:** Think about how old your children are, since that may impact the schedule you create or your ability to manage the nesting. For example, younger children usually need more frequent times with each parent.

2. **Their current state of mind:** How are the children managing now? Have your children shown signs that the family stress has affected them? These signs might be more clinginess, behavioral problems at home or at school, regression in sleep habits, or even physical symptoms, such as frequent stomachaches. Some children appear to be coping well at home but show signs of distress at school, or vice versa. Nesting provides a period of calm and stability that can help children adjust to their parents' separation. Parents who are nesting are able to reassure their children that both parents will still be with them, just not at the same time (they aren't losing a parent). It is also reassuring to them that there won't be abrupt or drastic changes. Life will go on more or less as it had before, at least for the nesting period.

3. **Their developmental needs:** While some kids, especially young children, need to see each parent frequently, other children find constant turnarounds unsettling and disruptive. If you believe it will help your older kids, consider a week-on/week-off schedule with a midweek visit with the off-duty parent. Most parents long to have some contact with their children during their off-duty time, especially if it's a longer stretch of time, and if it works for your children and your co-parent, include this in your schedule.

4. **Their relationships with each of you:** Are your children comfortable with both parents? Has there been tension or conflict between a parent and one or more of the children? If so, can you both focus on repairing that relationship? If one parent has been a less involved parent, it may take some time for your children to adjust to him or her becoming more actively involved. Remember, unless there is a compelling reason not to (such as abuse and/or neglect, which would rule out nesting as an option), children do best when they have a secure relationship with each of you.

5. **Any special needs:** If your child's abilities require certain accommodations, factor those in. I worked with a family with a severely disabled child, and the home had been adapted at great expense for her needs. The equipment needed for this child was extremely heavy, and much was permanently installed in the home. In addition, all changes were very upsetting for her, and her parents knew she would suffer if she had to move between two homes. Nesting made sense for this family. Another example is a child with special dietary needs. One parent might need to be brought up to speed in preparing these foods, but nesting is still possible.

6. **Any special newborn circumstances, such as breastfeeding:** If you have a child still breastfeeding, nesting is still an option. Parents can construct a schedule that allows nursing to continue for some time. Because it is so important for fathers and their children to develop strong attachments, and especially critical during the baby's first year, I encourage parents to find a way to make nesting work.

Thinking about these main considerations can help you assess your particular situation before you move forward. Later in this book, in Chapter 3, we'll see how to design a comprehensive co-parenting plan that addresses issues like these and boosts the success of your nesting.

CASE IN POINT

Jack and Allie's concerns about the impact of their separation on their children, nine-year-old Kate and twelve-year-old Sophie, led them to consider nesting. "Kate has been coming in to sleep with us every night," Allie told me. "She hasn't done that in years."

"Sophie's always been such a cheerful and independent kid with lots of her own friends from school," Jack went on. "But now she spends all day in her room with her headphones on. Her grades are down, and she doesn't want to bring her friends from school home anymore."

We realized that Kate and Sophie were anxious and needed to see their parents often, so Allie and Jack started with a rotation every three days. Over the following months, as their children adjusted, they stretched the rotations to five days and then to a week, adding a midweek visit with the off-duty parent.

Your Home Away from Home: Potential Living Arrangements

One of the major considerations in nesting is the ability to work out suitable living arrangements for all parties. Obviously, there is a financial angle underlying this decision. Following is information on the options available to you, their pros and cons, and what to think about as you make a choice.

FINDING A SPACE THAT WORKS

Here are some of the most common housing arrangements for the off-duty nesting parent. You and your partner will need to consider, without pressure or judgment, which option(s) is feasible and would work out the best for everyone.

Staying with Friends or Family

PROS: inexpensive

CONS: lack of privacy

Living in a room of someone else's house when off duty is an affordable way to nest. Of course, it requires sharing space with a family member or friend, which can work out well…but can also be potentially stressful depending on your relationship.

Sharing Space in the Family Home

PROS: inexpensive

CONS: lack of privacy, confusion for children

Some families decide to utilize a section of the family home, such as a guest bedroom, in-law unit, or separate floor of the home for the off-duty parent if they have the luxury of extra space.

An in-home separation with a clear understanding of the rules and guidelines can help parents find some respite and reduce their conflict. During the recession of 2008, many people who wanted to divorce simply could not afford to separate. Many chose to continue to share the family home while creating some separation between them. Even today, some rental markets are so expensive that it may not make financial sense to rent separate sites.

The advantages of sharing a home are that there is a minimal additional cost and the off-duty parent is available in an emergency. It is usually the least expensive option.

Sharing in-home space in the family home is less expensive, but it can also increase parents' stress thanks to the logistics that need to be managed. For example, a nesting couple working with me decided that both of them would remain in the home. They chose to negotiate specific times when the off-duty parent could use the kitchen. This turned out to be not only difficult to schedule but also confusing for the children. How could they figure out who was off duty or not available to them if they saw both parents in the kitchen at one time or another?

CASE IN POINT

Living together in one house can be the most financially prudent choice, but it does create other challenges. For example, Ted, a handyman, created a living space for the off-duty parent in an unused area of the basement. It worked well for him but was not as ideal for his wife.

"It doesn't give me the privacy or the relief from Ted's being around all the time that I need," she complained to me after trying it for a week. I reminded them that they could revisit their arrangement at any time and that it would take some time to adapt to any arrangement.

Ted and his wife discussed ways that he could be less intrusive. For example, he had been wandering into the kitchen when she was feeding their children. He hadn't realized how upsetting this was for her and the children. He agreed to make an effort to give her more privacy when she was on duty. He also moved more of his personal possessions, such as his clothing, to the basement. Finally, he agreed to shower after she had left to take the children to school. They were able to nest for several months, and then they found a studio apartment they could sublet and share for a few more months.

Sharing a Small Rented Apartment

PROS: clearer for children

CONS: somewhat expensive, lack of privacy

Off-duty parents can share a rented apartment—whoever is off duty lives there. This is up a level of potential expense, but it might be manageable since you're splitting the cost. Whether it is sustainable depends on how well you and your spouse are able to work respectfully together. And you will probably have more direct contact with your spouse. How will this feel? How important is it for you to have complete separation and respite? The right answers are the ones that are true for you. If you do decide to share a rented apartment, take the time to negotiate a written agreement and specific rules ahead of time. For example:

- Talk about whether each person should leave the apartment before the other comes in.
- Discuss household chore arrangements: Should dishes be washed and put away? How often will bed linens be cleaned?
- Is it acceptable to bring dates back to the apartment?

Communicating about how you'll handle issues like these *before* you start sharing a space can help you and your partner/roommate avoid conflicts down the road.

Renting a Room in Shared Housing

PROS: clearer for children, less expensive than renting an apartment, companionship

CONS: lack of privacy (e.g., shared bathrooms or kitchen)

If you decide to rent a room in a shared housing situation, other privacy complications can arise. You should think about how it would feel for you to live in a house with new roommates at this stage in your life. For some it might feel like an adventure; for others, it may feel uncomfortable. When my ex and I nested, I rented a room in a large five-bedroom house. I got along well with my four roommates and enjoyed my off-duty time at that home. I found that I had the privacy of my own room when I needed it, and the companionship of others in the shared living spaces. Perhaps it was easier for me to set boundaries with my roommates since they were not friends or family.

Renting an Off-Site Space for Each Parent

PROS: full privacy and independence

CONS: most expensive option

This is the costliest option, but it might work for some couples. Check out the rental market in your area to see what is available, what it would cost, and if it will fit your budget. The closer you are to the home where your children live, the easier nesting will be.

If one or both parents rent an apartment, they'll enjoy the highest level of privacy. Plus, nesting might feel more manageable when you have your own place to return to. However, again, this option can be costly and comes at a time when many spouses facing a long-term separation or divorce are worried about finances. You would both need to agree on the expenditure and weigh the costs and the benefits.

LOCATION OF THE HOUSING

If the off-duty parent will be staying somewhere other than the family home, it's important to consider the location. If your off-duty housing is near the family home, it will be easier to have frequent rotations, which is much better for very young children. On the other hand, living in a place that's *too* close might feel uncomfortable, depending on your needs for privacy. One guideline that has helped my clients is to locate your off-duty housing between two and seven miles of the family home. Beyond that, consider your proximity to the following:

- **The children's school:** Is it important to be able to stay in or very close to your children's school district when off duty? Involvement with your children's school life and activities is simpler when your off-duty home is close to their school. It benefits the children when both parents are actively involved with the children's school life.

- **Your job location:** Commute times and access to public transit if necessary will be everyday realities you'll need to face, so be sure to factor them in.

No matter where you choose to live, it might be a good idea to show your children the space at some point. They might want to visit your off-duty home to be able to picture their parents' lives when they are not in the family home.

CASE IN POINT

Sometimes despite your best efforts, location challenges make nesting impossible. Charles, a urological surgeon, took a new job in Florida near his aging parents. Emily and their children wanted to stay in the family home in Illinois. Both Emily and Charles felt that their children would do best if they could remain in the same city as their school, friends, and community.

After considering various travel schedules to try to accommodate nesting, Emily and Charles concluded that nesting wouldn't work for them. Instead, their children spent summer vacations with Charles, who visited them in Illinois as often as his work allowed.

Financial Factors

Financial feasibility is one of the first concerns most of my clients raise when we discuss nesting. If the nesting agreement creates too much financial stress, it probably will not be sustainable. Family incomes rarely increase during a family crisis, separation, or divorce. In fact, your income may decrease during a stressful time because your productivity may decline. You may not be able to work the overtime hours you have worked in the past. You may need to cut back your work to be able to care for your children or attend legal meetings.

When considering the ideal arrangement for your family, it is important to try to anticipate what increased expenses you might expect. For example, you may:

- Have legal expenses or increased counseling costs.
- Need to take unpaid time off from work to attend to parenting time or divorce proceedings.
- Have to furnish a second residence and pay additional living expenses.

How will expenses like this be paid? You and your spouse will also need to make decisions together as to how the home and children's expenses will be paid:

- Will you set up a separate family account? If so, how will it be funded?
- How important is it to each of you to track your expenses?
- How will you establish a budget?
- Do you need to establish guidelines about what expenses are legitimate home and children's expenses?

You may need to consult your accountant, if you have one, or hire a financial specialist to help you with these questions. We'll dig deeper into money questions in Chapter 4, where you'll see that creating a budget is both important and not as complicated as you might fear. For now, just look at your big-picture financial situation to decide if nesting is in the realm of possibility.

In many divorces, the family home is the single biggest asset, and it will need to be sold in order to complete the divorce settlement. Even if the home needs to be sold right away, a short period of nesting is still helpful to your children and you. A single transitional month of nesting will help your family stabilize. Even a short nesting period can still help you create a balanced, predictable time-share plan that supports your kids after you move to separate homes.

CASE IN POINT

When Hal and Susan considered nesting, financial realities became an obstacle right away. They couldn't afford to rent two off-duty sites *and* pay for their family home—but Hal wanted to begin dating immediately, so he really wanted a private living situation. They decided to sell their home and rent two apartments that were only a few blocks apart in the same neighborhood.

They agreed to nest just until their home sold, which ended up being about six months. In the interim, they found a realtor and took care of some deferred maintenance. They were able to prepare the children for the sale of the home and tried to build some excitement about the move to the new apartments. In the meantime, each parent became more confident of his or her single-parenting skills. Their cooperation in preparing the home for sale set a foundation of cooperative parenting postdivorce. In fact, they went together to look at apartments because they wanted their children to feel equally comfortable at both new sites. Hal told me that having had the experience of moving in and out of their "nest," he was much more patient and understanding of their children's experience as they "backed and forthed" after their move.

Dating and New Relationships

If you and/or your spouse are dating other people or want to, that decision can affect your ability to nest. Sometimes divorces happen because one of the parents has begun a new relationship. If there has been an affair, emotions will probably be volatile. In other situations, especially if the marriage has been "empty" for some time, one or both parents may be eager to start dating.

If your dating or new relationship can be completely separate from your on-duty parenting time, you may still be able to nest. (If the new relationship does not succeed, you will save your children from another loss by not telling them about it early on. We will talk more about this topic in Chapter 3.) My experience tells me that the issue of dating and new relationships can trigger very painful conflict, so it's critical to discuss and agree on these issues in your plan before you begin nesting. We will talk more about this in Chapter 3 when you write your agreement.

Should you choose to marry or have more children, nesting will certainly end at that point.

CASE IN POINT

Olivia and Barb had been living together for six years when it became legal for them to marry. They had adopted twin boys from a war-torn country in Africa and had co-parented well together. Eventually, Olivia began to drift away from the marriage and fell in love with another woman.

When we discussed nesting, they understood that the now eight-year-old twins would handle the divorce better if both parents could agree to put the kids' needs first. The boys had already experienced the trauma of losing their parents in Africa, so Olivia and Barb were determined to minimize any further stress for the boys.

Olivia struggled with guilt, although she wanted to leave their marriage. Barb was angry and grieving but accepted the reality of their separation and divorce. Fortunately, they were able to use time in therapy to work through these emotions, and Olivia agreed to keep her new relationship completely separate from their children for at least a year. Had Olivia been unable to make this agreement, nesting would likely have failed.

How Long Should Nesting Last?

Sharing the nest is usually temporary, for example for a few months until parents either reconcile or are further along in the divorce process when decisions about the home and the time-share schedule are made. Other parents may nest for several years. I have interviewed families that nested for as long as twelve years! Occasionally parents agree to nest even after divorce, until a milestone is reached, such as their children's graduation from high school.

So, there's no one set length that nesting should be. You might not be able to predict how the nesting period will unfold, so try to keep an open mind at this early stage. You might find that the coming and going, packing and unpacking that's part of nesting becomes stressful. Or you might find that a new relationship has become serious and you want to end nesting and move toward a more stable living situation. Or you might find that the situation works well for the children and you do it for longer than you imagined. The bottom line: At some point, one or both of you will likely be ready to end it.

You will ultimately nest for as long as it feels right for you and your partner. No matter how long people nested, nearly all reported back to me that they gained profound empathy for their children's experience of going back and forth from one parent's house to the other's house. Experiencing it yourself will help you understand your children's experiences and needs.

Nesting Deal Breakers

These are some situations where nesting might not be a workable choice for you, even if you have the best intentions. Be honest with yourself as you think these through.

IF YOU AND YOUR SPOUSE FIGHT A LOT

If you and your partner are separating, arguing might have become a big part of your relationship. More intense types of fights, however, could indicate that nesting will be very difficult. Are the arguments heart pounding, loud, frequent, and nasty? Are there threats, name-calling, or insults? Do the arguments feel out of control? Do they upset your children? These "high-conflict" relationships are not suitable for nesting. If your conflicts are more manageable, if you can keep them away from your kids, and if disagreements can be resolved before they rise to the level of high conflict, nesting is probably an option.

Remember, nesting requires good-enough communication and cooperation to be successful. If your arguments are unmanageable, nesting will not be healthy for you or your kids. In those cases, it's better for everyone to find a way to end the conflict, and full separation is most likely the right next step.

IF EITHER OF YOU ABUSES DRUGS OR ALCOHOL

Your children need a sober parent present in case of an emergency. If either or both of you are using drugs or alcohol to excess, nesting will surely fail. Kids need stable and sober parents in order to feel safe and secure, especially if they have had upsetting experiences of seeing their parents intoxicated or incapacitated. In situations where ongoing addiction has been part of the unraveling of the marriage, nesting is unlikely to work.

In high-conflict divorces, accusations of addiction, abuse, or mental illness often come up in custody battles. Sometimes these claims are true, and sometimes they are manipulative to get more custody time. Families involved in these types of conflicts cannot nest successfully.

If you or your spouse have been in recovery for a long time, however, and sobriety is a high priority to you both, then you might be able to construct a nesting agreement that supports your sobriety, as well as your family.

CASE IN POINT

I worked with a young couple who were both in recovery and had young children. Fran and Phillip had met at AA meetings and fallen in love, sharing their sobriety efforts and supporting each other in the twelve-step program. Their experiences with relapse differed, though. Fran repeatedly relapsed, while Phillip stayed sober. Both were committed parents and very much wanted their marriage to work, but Phillip was at his wit's end. Fran went to rehab again and again, and eventually Phillip decided to pursue separation.

Even as they discussed a separation, it was clear that the love was still there. In order to support her sobriety while ensuring the kids' safety, they created a nesting arrangement that prioritized sober parenting time for Fran and kept her involved as a parent. Initially, Phillip stayed in the family home, while Fran moved to her parents' house. When she came to the family home for time with their children, she agreed to be breathalyzed at the start and end of her on-duty time there.

Nesting started with Phillip being present during her one-day visits, then increasing her time alone with the kids on a pre-agreed-upon timeline and transitioning to overnights with their children as she remained sober. Phillip no longer felt he needed to supervise her.

Fran and Phillip agreed that it was important for Fran to be a fully involved, sober parent, and they worked toward sharing time equally over the next eight months with the understanding that if she relapsed, she would have to start over with the one-day visits. Because Fran and Phillip still loved each other, they were able to reconcile after a year of nesting and Fran's continued sobriety.

IF THERE HAS BEEN RECENT VIOLENCE

Safety for you and your children has to be your most important priority. Domestic violence, or what is also called "intimate partner violence," creates a severe and traumatic lack of safety for the entire family and means that nesting is not a good option.

If there has been recent violence, in the past year, for example, find help to establish a safe arrangement for you and your children instead of considering nesting. You might need legal restraining orders or court-mandated treatment for the abuser and for your children. Keep in mind that abusers often feel that they have nothing left to lose if a relationship ends and may resort to more or escalated violence. Focus on safety first and foremost.

If there was an episode of violence years before, and not since, nesting might be possible. The key is that the violence must have been addressed thoroughly, for example through therapy.

IF THERE ARE OTHER FORMS OF ABUSE

Nesting will not work in the presence of other forms of abuse, either. These other forms of abuse include coercive, controlling behavior; verbal threats and attacks; sexual abuse; and fiduciary abuse. In these situations, there's no "level playing field." One person has all the power, which makes it impossible to work cooperatively and with mutual respect to create a safe nest for your children.

CASE IN POINT

Janet came to me after making a hard decision to leave her husband, Eric. She wanted to nest to help their child through their divorce. However, despite being married for fifteen years, she had no access to their money or knowledge of their financial situation, and Eric was unwilling to share the information. "Eric gave me an allowance," she explained. He paid all the bills and pressured her to sign legal documents that she didn't understand.

This is an example of coercive control and fiduciary abuse. I asked her if she trusted Eric or if she thought he would become more open about their finances. "I doubt he will ever change," she said. "It never really bothered me before, but now that we are separating, I will never know if he's being completely open with me." Nesting requires parents to share financial information. Managing the children's and home expenses is a shared requirement. I could not recommend nesting in this case, because Eric's abuse would have kept Janet out of key financial decisions.

IF THERE IS UNCONTROLLED MENTAL ILLNESS

While intense emotions during separation or divorce are certainly normal, "uncontrolled mental illness" means a mental illness that impairs the ability to parent. If one of you is unstable because of untreated mental illness, nesting will not be a good choice, because children need stable parents. For example, if a depressed person cannot work for long stretches of time or attend regular treatment appointments, he or she is probably not able to care for children alone. Being a solo, on-duty parent is stressful, especially in the early stages of a separation or divorce. In addition, the stress of a separation could even worsen symptoms.

However, if a mental illness has been stabilized with medication or other treatments, nesting can be considered. If the mental illness is not affecting the parent's ability to care for the children and take responsibility for the home, nesting is possible.

A final note: Avoid trying to diagnose mental illness if you are not a professional (and do not accept a layperson's diagnosis of you). In high-conflict divorces, some parents will sometimes accuse each other of being a "narcissist" or a "borderline." Unless the person has been evaluated and definitively diagnosed by a qualified mental health professional, it's more likely that the conflict revolves around behaviors that the other parent finds upsetting or simply doesn't like.

IT JUST ISN'T A GOOD FIT FOR YOU

Nesting isn't for everyone. It might not be a good fit for you because of your history, your background, or your beliefs. For example, some couples have one parent who prefers to be the primary caregiver and one who prefers being far less involved—in those cases, nesting is probably not a good idea. Some cultural or religious beliefs might lead a couple to dismiss nesting. If you and your partner have special circumstances that will make nesting extremely difficult, taking the time to recognize and acknowledge them now is a better idea than trying to nest when you're not set up for success.

CASE IN POINT

Sophia and Daniel married in Mexico before immigrating to the United States. Sophia was a stay-at-home mom while Daniel found work in construction. Daniel worked long hours, and Sophia took care of the children and their small home. Sophia and Daniel were practicing Catholics; family and community were very important to them.

Gradually, Daniel began to integrate into mainstream culture, learned English, became restless, and began to pull away from his marriage and family. Sophia believed her role was to enforce tradition, morality, and religious values. She had no interest in separating from the Hispanic community in which she felt comfortable. Although divorce is less common in the Latino culture, Daniel yearned for his freedom.

I did not introduce the idea of nesting to Sophia and Daniel for several reasons. First, Daniel had not been a very involved parent. He understood his role to be providing for his family and that Sophia was the primary parent. He wouldn't be comfortable in a nesting arrangement. He preferred to give financial support to Sophia, who continued to be the primary parent. Second, Sophia's role as the primary parent gave her life meaning. She would feel lost during off-duty time. She leaned on her local community for emotional support and worked hard to preserve her own traditional values and culture.

Making a Decision

Now that you know how nesting works and the factors to consider before jumping in, you're probably pretty clear about whether nesting is right for your family. Ideally, both you and your spouse will read this book and reach an agreement together.

In the following chapters, we will explore many other questions, such as various nesting arrangements and how to tailor them to your family's unique situation and needs. You'll also find tools to help you support the nesting process through good communication, respectful decision-making, making and keeping agreements, and trust-building. The next chapters will guide you through all of these tasks, step-by-step.

KEY POINTS TO REMEMBER

- Assess your own ability to co-parent with the questionnaire and discuss with your spouse, looking carefully for any "red flags."

- Consider both the pros and cons of nesting for your family. Is nesting a good fit for all parties?

- You will need good-enough communication, flexibility, and trust. Are you both willing to cultivate these qualities? These are the cornerstones of nesting successfully.

- You'll need to set aside your emotions to focus on the children.

- While not required, do you want to have occasional "family time," such as weekly dinners? If so, are you both able to be comfortable together?

- Your parenting schedule is how you share time with your children. Ideally, it should minimize the disruption to your children and should be based on what will work for you, your work schedules, and your children's schedules. It should also maximize the time your children have with each parent.

- Work with your spouse to create a nesting arrangement that takes your kids' needs into account: their age and developmental needs, their current emotional state, and any special needs or circumstances.

- Find a space for your off-duty time that meets your needs. For example, you may need privacy or independence. Consider the type of space you can accept, such as a single room, staying with friends, or an apartment. Is it realistic to share a space with your spouse? The location of your off-duty space should work with your job location, your commute, your children's school, and proximity to the family home.

- Evaluate what is financially feasible and will work with your budget. You'll need basic agreements about how the house will be cared for and how expenses will be paid.

- Nesting is not recommended in some situations. These nesting deal breakers include issues such as ongoing conflict, violence, sexual or fiduciary abuse, abuse of drugs or alcohol, or untreated mental illness.

CHAPTER 3

Developing a Co-Parenting Plan

Once you know that nesting might be a good fit for you and your partner, it's time to focus on how to co-parent together. Co-parenting is a process where two parents partner to raise a child even though they are divorced or separated and do not live together. Given the fact that you and your partner probably won't spend much time together once you start nesting, working out a co-parenting plan ahead of time will help you work out points of contention, anticipate problems, and present a united front to your children. The parenting plan serves as a record of parenting decisions when future disagreements arise, while nesting and after, protecting your children from the stress of parental strife. We will start with your "mission" or "vision" statement that will help guide your decisions, agreements, and behaviors, then move on to making specific decisions about the kids' lives. Writing down this plan will help you keep everything organized—this chapter will walk you through the process, step-by-step.

This plan isn't set in stone—you and your partner may need to revise and tailor it to your family's needs. This plan is very comprehensive, but it's well worth your time and effort because it provides a strong foundation for your co-parenting during *and* after nesting. If you move on to divorce, your parenting plan (revised in any ways necessary) may be filed with the court along with the final divorce paperwork, or marital settlement agreement.

Managing Different Co-Parenting Styles

You and your partner might have had different parenting styles while you were a couple—that's a very common situation. While nesting, these differences can create confusion if you aren't clear about your overall parenting strategy. Now that you and your spouse will have new roles as single parents, working in tandem and coordinating your parenting when possible, communication about your parenting styles is paramount.

Finding common ground in parenting styles can be a challenge, but many couples are able to achieve it. As you start the nesting process, think of you and your partner on a continuum that describes how often you would like to coordinate with your co-parent on parenting choices. At one end of this continuum is the 100 percent co-parenting style, which describes parents who want to work closely together in all aspects of parenting. They want to agree about everything from bedtime routines, chores, discipline, screen time, whether the child can have a cell phone or an allowance, and what TV shows are acceptable. You might see yourself near that end of the continuum because you believe that consistency in child-rearing is very important and believe it will be easier for your children when both parents have the same rules and expectations. You will have to communicate a lot if this level of consistency is your goal.

On the other end of the spectrum are parents who want more of a "firewall" between them. Those parents want as little contact as possible with their spouse, perhaps because they feel they will get triggered every time they communicate. They may see their ex as intrusive or controlling, or might believe that they will minimize fighting if they are not trying to agree on every tiny thing. Generally, you will have to communicate less often with your partner if you're on this end of the spectrum. Most parents fall somewhere between these two extremes.

While it's possible to nest no matter where you fall on the continuum, it's important to know where you stand so you can manage your expectations. Will you come to an agreement on all choices? Or will the information and communication between you and your spouse be reduced to what you see as the bare minimum required to make nesting work?

WHERE DO EACH OF YOU FALL?

Make an X on the place on the continuum where you see yourself, and have your partner do the same. Marking your individual spots will help you figure out where you and your spouse may be able to meet somewhere between them on that continuum in order to minimize conflict. There is a "sweet spot" on the continuum between where you two marked that allows for good parenting without conflict. Even if there seems to be a big discrepancy when you first mark your spots, you might be able to negotiate some compromises in order to make the nesting successful. Or you may have to accept that your differing parenting styles will carry over into the nesting. That's okay, too, because children will adjust as long as the conflict is minimal.

MEETING IN THE MIDDLE

Don't feel discouraged if you seem to have varied styles or your marks seem far apart—but think about how much compromise is realistic. Parents are often in a power struggle regarding their different parenting styles. This even might be one of the issues that led you and your spouse to separate in the first place. One parent might view the other as incompetent or simply not a very good parent. One parent might try to make up for the deficiencies of the other by, for example, being very strict when the other parent is seen as too laissez-faire. As in any negotiation, be willing to see the other person's viewpoint but hold on to your core principles. Think of this nesting period as a stepping-stone to help you two transition to fully separate parenting. You might need to give up a little of the control you're used to, or you might need to cooperate more than you have in the past. Either way, keep your main goal in mind: to minimize stress on the children.

Generally, one parent ends up closer to the parallel parenting end of the continuum. If you can accept this, you will have less conflict between partners, which is a key goal of both separating and nesting. The reduction or absence of conflict is also vital to your children's well-being.

CO-PARENTING VIA COMPROMISES

Once you've come to an agreement on how much cooperation you expect to have on parenting decisions, you can move on to creating a co-parenting plan. The rest of this chapter will cover issues about which you'll need to think, discuss, and reach a conclusion. Your parenting styles will influence your decisions on many issues, but now that you have thought about how closely you and your spouse can collaborate, you are in a better mindset to compromise when needed. The list might seem overwhelming at first, so take it one piece at a time. (In addition to the worksheet in this book, you will find many different parenting plan worksheets on the Internet that will walk you through many of the questions.) You may find that you and your spouse already agree on many of the issues.

The Mission Statement

One way to start your co-parenting plan is to talk about your shared vision for your family during nesting, separation, and divorce. Some parents think of this as a "mission statement." You two will write this statement together, and it will provide the reference point for all of the many decisions you will consider in your co-parenting plan. The vision or mission statement is designed to ensure that your nesting and parenting decisions fit the goals that you both have agreed to.

The vision or mission statement is a positive, hopeful, and sincere forecasting of how you will work as co-parents. You can include communication goals and personal goals. You may also want to describe the quality of the relationship you hope to have with each other over the long term. Many parents also set the foundation for creating a solid nesting agreement by describing and ranking each parent's long- and short-term intentions related to the divorce process, parenting, and emotions. Since this document is one that is not usually shared with your children, these statements will help remind you of what really matters to each of you. (You could share this statement with older children if it is positive and helpful.) For example, if one of you envisions a time when you may be friends and able to celebrate holidays together with your children, your spouse may not now (or ever) necessarily agree with that goal. However, you can include these goals in your vision or mission statement to help you with your decision-making as you discuss your longer-term parenting plan.

Here's an example of one couple's co-parenting mission statement:

We love our children unconditionally and want to show them every day in our words and actions. We want our children to feel loved, cherished, respected, and understood by both of us. We want our children to know that we will work together to help them with school, their social lives, and every other aspect of their lives as they grow up.

We will make mistakes, at times, but will always try to repair them. We want our children to know that it's perfectly okay to make mistakes as well, and that they can learn how to apologize and learn from their own mistakes. We will work together when discipline is necessary, and never resort to any kind of violence. It is important to us that our children feel safe, loved, supported, and protected by both of us.

We want our children to learn the values we hold important, such as honesty, self-reliance, learning, integrity, and respect for others. We believe that good, honest, and respectful communication is always important, and would like our chil-

dren to grow up knowing that they can count on this from both parents. We believe that education and learning, both in and out of school, is important, and we will encourage and support our children as they pursue their interests and dreams.

It is our goal to work together peacefully to give our children a foundation upon which to build their own successful lives, in their future relationships, education, and careers. We hope to be able to celebrate all of their successes together with them.

As you can see, the vision or mission statement will be unique to your family. It is important to describe your vision as well as you can, with as much detail as possible.

Scheduling Time with the Children

Deciding which parent will be with the children when is one of the main considerations in co-parenting. This section will outline how to decide on a schedule that works for you, taking into account important holidays and events during the year. You should also document the ways in which you will deal with unplanned changes in the regular schedule.

DAY-TO-DAY SCHEDULING

You and your partner should consider your work schedules, other responsibilities, and personal preferences, as well as your children's needs, as you build a regular schedule for who will care for the children. This schedule could look one way during the nesting period and a different way after it, or it could stay the same. Keeping a shared online calendar can help you keep all of these dates straight.

EXTRACURRICULAR AND SOCIAL ACTIVITIES

If your children are involved in extracurricular activities, document your decisions about how those will be handled. If your budget allows, try to continue your children's activities to ensure the stability of their schedules and social lives. It's important, however, to avoid any commitment that intrudes on the other parent's time with your children, unless you have a clear agreement to do so. For example, if a child is invited to a birthday party during your partner's scheduled time, your partner will decide whether the child will attend the party.

If your children are older, you'll need an agreement about how you'll decide whether they can attend social activities, parties, and so on. Does the on-duty parent decide alone? Does the off-duty parent need to be consulted in all or certain circumstances?

HOLIDAYS, BIRTHDAYS, AND SCHOOL VACATIONS

Holidays, birthdays (parents' and children's), and school vacations are typically exceptions to the default schedule you have established. Think about how your family has celebrated holidays and other traditions in the past and which traditions you would like to keep while you nest. Ask yourselves these questions:

- How comfortable would you be celebrating these events with your ex?

- Would you prefer to divide the holidays and vacations equally, or would you rather choose the holidays that mean the most to you?

- Will three-day weekends trump your regular schedule, or would you rather keep the default schedule?

- How will you treat birthdays in the schedule? Would you like to see your children on their birthdays if you are off duty? Who will plan their birthday parties?

- You'll need to decide how to divide winter and spring school breaks. Some divide the days and others alternate each year.

- You'll need to have an agreement that includes holidays (including both days of multiday holidays, such as Christmas Eve and Christmas Day).

The worksheets at the end of this chapter will help you divide up specific holidays.

Summer Vacations

Families often plan camps, travel, and other activities during the summer months. Because camps often fill up early, you should agree to meet and confirm your schedule at least three or four months before the end of the school year, if not more, depending on your area. Decide whether to keep the regular schedule during the summer or modify it to accommodate your summer plans.

Parents often want longer periods of time to travel with their children in the summer. Document your agreements about how much time will work for each of you. Often parents agree that each may take the children for up to two or three consecutive weeks in the summer, and each parent gets the first choice of dates for travel in alternate years. Like camp plans, vacation plans often need to take form well in advance of the summer, so be sure to have this discussion early enough that there are no surprises.

UNDERSTANDING "RIGHT OF FIRST CARE"

When you make a schedule, all time will be accounted for—meaning, your children will always be with one parent or the other. Of course, life happens, and sometimes the scheduled parent cannot be with the children for one reason or another. As a psychologist, I know that children are happier and healthier when they are with one of their parents, so I urge you to make an agreement in your co-parenting plan about when one of you must notify the other that you're not available, in order to give a parent the chance to jump in and be with your children before you arrange childcare with a friend, family member, or babysitter.

The legal term for this is "right of first refusal" and often referred to as the "right of first care." It means that you agree to offer the other parent the opportunity to care for your children when you can't be on duty, and your co-parent has the option to accept or not. If your co-parent isn't able to step in, then the on-duty parent is responsible for finding alternate care. Two important questions arise in this situation:

1. What period of time triggers this mandate? A certain number of hours?
2. How much advance notice do you have to give your co-parent?

If you have younger children, you might agree that the mandate becomes effective when you know the on-duty parent will be away for more than three or four hours. You always have the option of inviting your co-parent to step in. It just doesn't become *required* until the agreed-upon time.

With older children, you might agree that the mandate would only be triggered when the on-duty parent will be absent for eight or twelve hours, or overnight. Think about your children's needs and what you believe will work best for them and for you.

Unfortunately, I have seen angry parents punish the other parent by withholding their option to step in and care for their children. It is important to remember that your children need you both and withholding the option (essentially preventing the other parent from caring for them) is hurtful to your children and to your co-parent. Acting out in anger at the expense of your children is not good parenting and will not build the trust you need to parent your children cooperatively.

CASE IN POINT

Hal and Susan, whom you may remember from Chapter 2, agreed to a four-hour mandate. Since their rented apartments were nearby, the children could ride their bikes from the home to the off-duty parent when they wanted to. Their nesting went well, until there was a glitch that could have unraveled the arrangement.

This happened when their children mentioned to Susan that Hal had a new babysitter who cared for them regularly when he was not home. Hal had not offered the opportunity to Susan, and she was angry about this. When they revisited their agreement, Hal realized his mistake, but he felt that four hours was simply too short a time. They changed the agreement to eight hours, and he recommitted to the agreement. In addition, they agreed that each of them would be invited to meet any new childcare providers so they would both know who was caring for their children in their absence.

Logistics Related to Your Children's Care

Outside of scheduling, you and your partner have several other areas of your children's lives to discuss. Following are some key topics.

EDUCATION

Ideally, your children can continue to attend the same school during your separation. If your children are in a private school, however, you may find that this is a place where you need to cut back expenses. Document your decision about this in your parenting plan.

Also, include agreements about participating together or separately in school activities, such as assemblies, field trips, concerts, or performances. Agree to note necessary school activities in your shared online calendar.

MEDICAL AND MENTAL HEALTHCARE

You'll need to document how you will make decisions regarding your children's healthcare. Who will be the primary liaison with medical professionals? If your child has special needs, any related specific circumstances should be addressed in your parenting plan.

When you travel, with or without your children, I recommend that you let your co-parent know how many hours you will be away in travel time. Emergencies may arise; what if one of your children becomes injured or ill? In a situation like this, both parents should be informed immediately.

If your child is sick or injured, and you know how long it will take the traveling parent to return home, you may either hold off on the child's treatment or confer by phone if possible. If you are traveling and will not have cell phone service, share your itinerary with your contact information. Even if one or both of you prefer a parallel parenting style, in an emergency it is best for your children to involve your co-parent.

You'll also need to agree that in a medical or mental health emergency, the parent on duty will give consent for treatment and inform the co-parent as soon as possible. You will need to check with your attorney or mediator since there may be laws in your jurisdiction regarding parental consent for treatment for separated or divorcing parents.

CULTURE AND RELIGION

It's common that parents have different religious or cultural backgrounds and that they made some decisions in their marriage about how the children would be raised. While you may have had some agreements around these issues in the past, you may feel differently now.

Decide whether your children will receive religious training or attend a place of worship. For example, you may agree that each of you can take your children to your own place of worship when you are on duty.

CASE IN POINT

If you initially run into obstacles scheduling holidays or events, try to find ways to work them out. Olivia and Barb, you may remember, adopted twins from Africa. They had participated in annual events celebrating their cultural heritage and wanted to continue to do so. They were active members of an African Heritage Cultural Arts Center and had traveled with their children every year to an African Heritage Festival. They agreed that this event was important for them and their children and that it was worth the expense. However, Barb didn't feel she could travel with Olivia now that they had separated. Instead, they agreed to take turns taking the kids every other year.

TRAVEL

Agree in your parenting plan who will store your children's passports and make them available upon request. Also, know that if a parent takes the child out of the country, one of you may need a written, notarized statement of permission from the other parent. (Consult with an attorney about the laws in your jurisdiction.) Also, some parents agree that they will be informed if the child goes out of the state.

CASE IN POINT

Brad and Emma had specific concerns. One of their children, William, was severely mentally handicapped and had specific regimens he'd follow for stress relief. When William fell at school and broke his arm, he wanted his father to be with him for comfort, but his father was away on business. Fortunately, Emma knew how to reach Brad, which she did right away. She also let William know that it would take some hours before Brad would be able to come home, but in the interim William was able to speak with his father on the phone.

If Brad had been away with William, however, and Emma had an accident, it would also be important for her to be able to reach Brad. She would need to give him notice that she would not be able to care for William for some time after they returned.

Driving

Make decisions about the children's driving privileges, including when or whether they can take drivers' training or get a license. Decide whether your child can have access to a car and, if so, how you will deal with the costs of a car and auto insurance. You may also want to make agreements about how far your child can travel alone or with friends without adult supervision.

OTHER IMPORTANT DECISIONS

This is where you tailor the plan to your family and your values and needs. Here are some topics parents choose to address:

- Agreements about abiding by the industry ratings of movies, video games, and TV shows
- Screen time, social media, and cell phone use
- Allowances, chores, and teen jobs
- Nutrition and diet
- Drug and alcohol use
- Dating
- Discipline
- Bedtimes

I urge parents to include explicit agreements about how they speak to their children about the other parent. Bad-mouthing the other parent forces your children into a loyalty bind, and we know from research that your children will do best if they can love both of you.

CASE IN POINT

If you remember Phillip and Fran from Chapter 2, you will recall that the nesting was conditional on Fran remaining sober. There had been times when Phillip was so frustrated with Fran's previous relapses that he was barely able to control what he said to their children. Part of their nesting agreement addressed this topic and outlined that Phillip would tell the kids that Fran was sick and getting treatment. They both hoped to reconcile, and Phillip did not want to turn their children against their mother.

New Relationships

Your co-parenting agreement should address how you and your partner will handle dating and new relationships. This sensitive topic comes up frequently with separating parties, and it should be handled thoughtfully and carefully.

While you're in the process of separating and nesting, no new relationship should be brought into the nesting home or the shared off-site location. My recommendation is to consider introducing your children to a new partner only after the divorce is finalized and the new relationship has become a committed relationship of some duration, ideally nine to twelve months.

THINK FIRST OF YOUR CHILDREN

Why be so strict about keeping new relationships separate from your children? The reason is that your children have already experienced one loss. If they become attached to your new partner, and that relationship ends, your children will endure another loss. I have seen the effects of serial losses on children in my work. These children have a very hard time accepting new people into their lives and will likely have difficulty attaching to relationships of their own as they grow up.

Also, your children are adjusting to a significant change in the family, probably mourning the loss of the united family that once inhabited the home. They're probably wishing their parents would stay together. They are certainly not ready to accept any of your new romantic partners.

There is a misguided belief among many divorcing parents that their children "want me to be happy." Another version of this myth is that they will be better parents if they are happy in a new relationship. "My mom got a lot happier after the divorce," one child said to me, "but the rest of us got unhappier." Parents who believe this are usually eager to bring the new partner into the family, often long before their children are ready to accept the new relationship. The new relationship often fails when the children reject the newcomer or begin to act out their feelings in other ways.

Children, especially younger children, are more concerned with their own happiness than their parents' happiness. Even adult children are profoundly affected by their parents' divorce and will need time before they will accept a new relationship.

TELL ONE ANOTHER BEFORE THE CHILDREN

I recommend that you agree to notify your ex before introducing your children to a new relationship. This will prevent his or her shock, dismay, or anger from erupting when he or she hears the news from your children. In other words, if your son tells you, "Daddy has a new girlfriend," you would be able to say, "I know, honey. Daddy told me about her and that you would be meeting her. How did it go?" instead of "He does?! Who?" A calm and informed reaction tells your children that their parents are working together and reassures them that you will be able to accept this news without any upset. Notifying your co-parent before introducing your children to a new partner should be written into your parenting plan.

Many parents agree to share information about how the children react to a new significant other. Children will often talk about "Daddy's new girlfriend" or "Mommy's new boyfriend" to their other parent. You can include your intention to share those conversations (in as objective and composed a manner as possible) as constructive feedback so that you both can track how your children are doing.

A further complication arises when the new relationship is someone known to the children. This might be a family friend, the parent of a playmate, or a teacher or sports coach. This needs to be handled very sensitively and probably with the help of a therapist.

CASE IN POINT

While Jennifer and Kurt didn't have an agreement about bringing new partners into their family home, Jennifer had assumed neither of them would do that. Kurt didn't know about Jennifer's assumptions and hadn't considered how this question might affect her or their children. When Jennifer discovered a used condom in their bedroom in the family home after Kurt had been on duty, she was furious because she felt like it was such a blatant insult to her. Then she thought about what Kurt may have exposed or said to the children and about how the children might have experienced or felt about Kurt's new girlfriend. Nesting abruptly came to an end.

Jennifer regretted that they had not taken the time to be more specific in their nesting agreement. Nevertheless, she felt the children had benefited from the nesting period, even though it was a shorter period than she had envisioned. As they moved toward divorce, she insisted on working with Kurt and a counselor to develop a detailed written postdivorce parenting plan, as discussed in Chapter 5, that clearly spelled out agreements and expectations regarding new relationships.

How to Handle Disagreements That Arise

Most of your decisions will be influenced by where you and your co-parent land on the co-parenting continuum discussed at the beginning of this chapter. I recommend that you have regular, periodic meetings to review your parenting plan, in person or by Skype, Facetime, or other video/audio connection. The purpose of "predeciding" these major issues is to prevent or minimize conflict.

That said, you'll never be able to include all of the myriad decisions you'll make as parents every day. If you and your co-parent have a disagreement about a decision not covered in your parenting plan, have a plan as to how to deal with it before it rises to the level of conflict. For minor issues, you might be able to talk and work it out yourselves, revisiting your co-parenting mission statement to center yourselves and guide your decisions. For larger problems that aren't easy to resolve, I suggest that you include something like this in your parenting plan:

Either parent may decide that mediation with a neutral third person, such as a mediator or therapist, is necessary. That parent will let the other know of this intention, and we both agree to attend the meeting as soon as possible.

> *The mediator will discuss the disagreement with each of us, with the goal of working out a mutually acceptable solution.*
>
> *In the event that the conflict involves an issue that is particularly time-sensitive (for example, a medical concern), we will take professional advice, obtain a second opinion, if that is necessary, and follow the most prudent course.*

Future disagreements or new unanticipated issues are inevitable. This is a mechanism to resolve them quickly and reasonably, protecting your children from the stress of escalating and destructive parental conflict.

Parenting Plan Worksheet

You can complete this worksheet, which I've adapted from Gary Direnfeld, MSW, RSW (www.yoursocialworker.com), and used with permission to facilitate your discussion and development of a parenting plan for use during your nesting period. Some of the following items will only be addressed or revised when nesting ends.

Date: ....

	Parent	Parent
Name		
Address		
City		
State, Zip		
Telephone		
Cell		
Email		

This plan has been developed through the following process:

....

....

CO-PARENTING MISSION STATEMENT

....

....

....

This parenting plan applies to the following children:

	Name	Birth Date
Child 1		
Child 2		
Child 3		
Child 4		
Child 5		

NESTING AGREEMENTS

While nesting, we will have the following financial arrangement to fund the child(ren)'s and home expenses:

....

....

....

While nesting, we agree to update each other on the child(ren) and home whenever going off duty. Specifically:

....

....

....

While nesting, we will commit to leaving the home in good condition when going off duty and will respect the privacy needs of both parents. Specifically:

....

....

....

While nesting, we agree to not bring dates or new relationships into the family home or any shared off-site residence.

....

....

Other:

....

....

....

....

....

....

....

ON-DUTY SCHEDULE

Key: Use your initials, "M" for mother and "F" for father, or some other notation to mark the boxes.

Week 1	Mon	Tues	Wed	Thu	Fri	Sat	Sun
Morning							
Afternoon							
Evening							
Night							

Week 2	Mon	Tues	Wed	Thu	Fri	Sat	Sun
Morning							
Afternoon							
Evening							
Night							

Description:

....

....

Location of pickups:

....

Location of drop-offs:

....

SCHEDULE FOR WINTER/CHRISTMAS VACATION

☐ .... ☐ .... will be on duty during the winter vacation, or .... will be on duty for the first week and .... for the second week of winter vacation in ☐ even ☐ odd years and the reverse in alternate years, or

☐ Other:

....

....

MIDWINTER BREAK

☐ .... ☐ .... will be on duty during the ski week, or .... will be on duty for the first week and .... for the second week of ski week in ☐ even ☐ odd years and the reverse in alternate years, or

☐ Other:

....

....

SCHEDULE FOR SPRING VACATION

☐ .... ☐ .... will be on duty during the spring vacation, or .... will be on duty for the first half and .... for the second half of spring vacation in ☐ even ☐ odd years and the reverse in alternate years, exchanging the child(ren) on this day: ...., or

☐ Other:

....

....

SUMMER SCHEDULE

Upon completion of the school year, our on-duty schedule will be as follows:

- Same as school year schedule
- One week every month
- Two weeks every month
- One month
- Other:

....

....

....

....

We will determine the dates for the summer schedule each year no later than: (date) ....

If we both desire the same time frame, ...'s choice shall be given greater weight in ☐ even ☐ odd years and ....'s choice shall be given greater weight in ☐ even ☐ odd years.

SCHEDULE FOR HOLIDAYS

The on-duty schedule for the child(ren) for the holidays is:

	Mother	Father	Odd Years	Even Years	Every Year
New Year's Day	☐	☐	☐	☐	☐
Martin Luther King Jr. Day	☐	☐	☐	☐	☐
Presidents' Day	☐	☐	☐	☐	☐
Easter Friday	☐	☐	☐	☐	☐
Easter Sunday	☐	☐	☐	☐	☐
Passover	☐	☐	☐	☐	☐
Mother's Day	☐	☐	☐	☐	☐
Memorial Day	☐	☐	☐	☐	☐
Father's Day	☐	☐	☐	☐	☐
Fourth of July	☐	☐	☐	☐	☐
Labor Day	☐	☐	☐	☐	☐
Rosh Hashanah	☐	☐	☐	☐	☐
Yom Kippur	☐	☐	☐	☐	☐

	Mother	Father	Odd Years	Even Years	Every Year
Columbus Day	☐	☐	☐	☐	☐
Thanksgiving Day	☐	☐	☐	☐	☐
Hanukkah	☐	☐	☐	☐	☐
Christmas Eve	☐	☐	☐	☐	☐
Christmas Day	☐	☐	☐	☐	☐
	☐	☐	☐	☐	☐
	☐	☐	☐	☐	☐
	☐	☐	☐	☐	☐
	☐	☐	☐	☐	☐
	☐	☐	☐	☐	☐
	☐	☐	☐	☐	☐
	☐	☐	☐	☐	☐
	☐	☐	☐	☐	☐
	☐	☐	☐	☐	☐
	☐	☐	☐	☐	☐
	☐	☐	☐	☐	☐
	☐	☐	☐	☐	☐

For purposes of this parenting plan, holiday times will begin and end as follows:

☐ Holidays that fall on a Friday or Monday will include Saturday and Sunday.

It is understood that holidays and vacations trump the regular schedule unless we agree otherwise.

BIRTHDAYS

Parents' Birthdays

Each of us will have the option of having the child(ren) for a
............-hour visit on our birthday if the child(ren) is/are not
already with the parent on that day. The timing of the visit shall
be arranged with at least .... days'/weeks' notice.

Child(ren)'s Birthdays

1. We will hold birthday parties for the child in alternating
   years, with .... holding the party in ☐ even
   ☐ odd years and .... holding the party in
   ☐ even ☐ odd years. The child(ren)'s birthdays are special
   days in themselves and supersede the regular parenting
   schedule.

2. The parent who holds the party will cover the expenses for
   the celebration. The nonhost parent is responsible only for
   his or her own present(s) for the child.

3. The nonhost parent may attend the birthday party with
   prior agreement.

4. The nonhost parent will be able to spend up to two hours
   with the child before 4:00 p.m. on the child's birthday,
   provided that this has been arranged with the other parent at
   least .... days/weeks in advance, in order to be convenient
   for both of us.

TRANSPORTATION ARRANGEMENTS

After we separate, transportation arrangements for the child(ren)
between us at the change of parenting schedule will be as follows:

- The parent ending her/his on-duty time with the child(ren) transports to the other parent whenever possible (post-nesting).

- ☐ .... ☐ .... always transports the child(ren), or

- Other:

  ....

  ....

  ....

SCHOOL/DAYCARE

Enrollment/Attendance

The child(ren) will be enrolled and attend as follows:

	School	Grade(s)
Child 1		
Child 2		
Child 3		
Child 4		
Child 5		

1. ☐ .... ☐ .... ☐ We both will live in the jurisdiction of the local school (when nesting ends).

2. The child(ren) shall continue to attend such schools and/or daycare as long as we agree.

3. In the event that the school authorities should find that a child might be an exceptional student or a student with spe-

cial needs, both of us will have the right to attend and be informed of any pertinent meetings or testing.

4. The consent of ☐ .... ☐ .... ☐ Both will be needed before any special recommendations can be instituted.

5. With the consent of the school, we will both be provided by the school with separate notices of events and report cards. In order that this provision might be carried out, we will provide the school with current contact information, including email and cell phone, for all communications during the year.

6. We both have the ability to share in the child(ren)'s school activities. We will both be informed of any school trips or activities in which parental participation is desired, and we will discuss among ourselves whether one or both of us will attend. If we are unable to decide which school-related activities we will attend, we will alternate with Mother taking the first activity day in even-numbered years and Father taking the first activity day in odd-numbered years.

7. ☐ .... ☐ .... shall be the primary liaison person with the school.

8. Prior to graduation from high school, we will consult with each other with respect to the post–high school education of the child(ren) and costs if not otherwise determined in our marital settlement agreement.

9. We agree on the following regarding any special education or tutoring:

....

....

RELIGIOUS/SPIRITUAL UPBRINGING

Will your children have religious training or attend a place of worship? If so, complete this section.

We agree that the child(ren) will attend ....
.... (place of worship), and we will continue, when possible, to attend with the child(ren). We agree to discuss future religious training at this place of worship at the appropriate age: ....

Other considerations:

- We may each take the child(ren) to our place of worship during our on-duty time. We agree that neither of us will undermine the other parent's observance of his or her religion with the child(ren).

- Neither of us may enroll the child(ren) in religious training without the consent of the other parent, or ☐ .... will decide on religious training if we are unable to agree.

EXTRACURRICULAR ACTIVITIES

We encourage the child(ren) to engage in the following extra-curricular activities:

	Name	Activity
Child 1		
Child 2		
Child 3		
Child 4		
Child 5		

- Costs for extracurricular activities to be shared as follows:
☐ .... ☐ .... ☐ Both equally, or

☐ Costs to be determined by our nesting agreement, and later in our marital settlement agreement.

- Other: ☐ ....

- To the extent that either of us is not willing to participate in the funding of any extracurricular activity, then the other parent will have the sole decision-making authority with respect to that activity and the non-funding parent will not object.

- There will be no comment made with respect to the financial non-contribution of one parent in the provision of extracurricular activities by the other.

- Neither of us will enroll a child in extracurricular activities that will result in the exclusion, whether intentional or unintentional, of the other without the consent of the other. Neither of us will commit a child to activities that interfere with the other parent's time with the child without consent.

- As our child(ren) enter(s) the teenage years, the child(ren) will be permitted to attend social functions sponsored by the school or church, as well as private parties, provided both parents are satisfied that alcohol and drugs are not available at those functions. We will consult each other regarding any such function and will, when possible, reach a joint decision on whether the child(ren) may attend.

- In the event that there is any disagreement with attendance in extracurricular activities or social functions, ☐ .... ☐ .... ☐ the on-duty parent will make the decision.

USE OF A CAR

We will consult regarding driving decisions, driving lessons, and insurance. If we are unable to reach an agreement, ☐ .... ☐ .... will make the decision.

PARENTAL BEHAVIOR

1. We will conduct ourselves with respect to each other and the child(ren) so as to provide a loving, stable, consistent, and nurturing relationship with the child(ren) even though we no longer cohabit. To that end, we will not speak derogatorily of each other or the members of the family of the other, will not cause the child(ren) to be drawn into any dispute regarding decisions affecting the child(ren), and will not attempt to curry favor with the child(ren) to the detriment of the other.

2. At all times we would like to model appropriate behavior and judgment regarding alcohol, smoking, drug use, and sexual and aggressive behaviors toward each other or others. We will make efforts to protect the child(ren) from exposure to abuses of the previously listed behaviors.

3. To this end, we agree to use alcohol or other substances ☐ only when off duty or ☐ only in moderation when on duty. At those times, we will ensure that there is at least one unimpaired adult present in case of an emergency involving the child(ren).

4. We agree not to drink and drive.

5. We agree to respect the prevailing rating systems regarding movies, music, TV, and video games.

EXPECTATIONS AROUND PARENTAL DATING AND NEW RELATIONSHIPS

1. We agree to protect the child(ren) from parental dating and new relationships. To that end, we will not introduce the child(ren) to a new relationship until it has become a committed relationship of .... duration. In addition, we agree to notify the other parent before the child(ren) are informed or introduced to a new relationship.

2. We will refrain from introducing the child(ren) to casual dates.

3. If either of us establishes a relationship with a person who is becoming a "significant other," we will inform the other parent, as soon as practicable, before introducing this person to the child(ren). The child(ren) may inadvertently meet or be introduced to a person who eventually may become a "significant other" to either of us. In this case, if either of us establishes a relationship with a person who may be known to our child(ren), before we introduce this person as a "significant other" to our child(ren), we will inform the other parent.

4. Child(ren) will be introduced to the significant other gradually with the initial introduction taking place in a neutral public setting.

5. We will use discretion in displaying signs of affection in front of our child(ren).

6. Overnight stays will not occur until it has been established our child(ren) are comfortable with the new relationship.

7. Feedback will be exchanged between us at any time and at intervals during the process of the introduction of a new close adult in our child(ren)'s life.

8. We will consider outside counseling support for our child(ren), if necessary, to aid in the adjustment to "significant others" in our child(ren)'s life.

9. Cohabitation, engagement, or plans to marry will be conveyed to the other parent before informing our child(ren), and it will be the right of the initiating parent to inform our child(ren).

10. We will discuss the role of the stepparent. We and the stepparent(s) will make every effort to foster a positive relationship between the stepparent(s) and the other biological parent. It will be expected that the stepparent(s) will leave the parenting and parenting decisions to us, the biological parents, with the exception of medical emergencies—at which point both biological parents will be contacted immediately.

11. Information and knowledge of half-sibs, pregnancies, or plans of adoption of siblings will be conveyed to the other parent before informing our child(ren), and it will be the right of the initiating parent to inform them.

12. We and future stepparent(s) will avail ourselves of stepparenting information.

DAY-TO-DAY DECISIONS

We will make decisions regarding the day-to-day care and control of each child while on duty. Regardless of the allocation of decision-making in the parenting plan, either of us may make emergency decisions affecting the health and safety of our child(ren).

MEDICAL

Our child(ren) will be medically cared for by the following primary care providers and additional providers who will be selected by ☐ .... ☐ .... ☐ Both parents.

	Physician	Telephone Number
Child 1		
Child 2		
Child 3		
Child 4		
Child 5		

	Dentist	Telephone Number
Child 1		
Child 2		
Child 3		
Child 4		
Child 5		

	Other	Telephone Number
Child 1		
Child 2		
Child 3		
Child 4		
Child 5		

1. We both have the right to give consent to emergency medical/dental care during times that we are on duty.

2. We will inform the other parent of the extent and nature of any emergency and treatment thereof as soon as it is reasonably possible.

3. The parent who is on duty when a child becomes ill will inform the other parent of the nature and extent of the illness as soon as it is practically possible.

4. We both have the right to be informed by the parent who schedules it and to attend any regular medical, dental, or orthodontic appointments that our child(ren) might have.

5. We both have the right to receive information from and give information to a medical professional (that includes other healthcare professionals, such as nurses, physiotherapists, social workers, psychologists, and others).

6. If each child needs to be referred to a medical or dental subspecialist, the consent of ☐ .... ☐ .... ☐ Both parents will be needed for such a referral.

7. ☐ .... ☐ .... shall be the primary liaison with each child's doctor.

8. ☐ .... ☐ .... shall be the primary liaison with each child's dentist.

9. ☐ .... ☐ .... shall be the primary liaison with each child's orthodontist.

10. If there should be a need for our child(ren) to be referred to a practitioner skilled in social, emotional, or behavioral problems, the consent of ☐ .... ☐ .... ☐ Both parents shall be needed for such a referral. Both of us have the absolute right to participate in, consult with, and be consulted by such a practitioner. The form that such participation or consultation should take will be left to the judgment of the clinician.

DAILY NEEDS

When on duty we will ensure that our child(ren) will be properly groomed, fed, clothed, and supervised. We will provide physical care, healthcare, and daycare as appropriate.

PARENTS' FUTURE HOUSING

After we separate to two homes, we agree to live within a ....-mile radius of each other or of this location:

....

....

TRAVEL

1. Our children's passport(s) will be stored by ...., but will be available upon request by the other parent.

2. We agree that our child(ren) will not be taken outside of the state of our residence without the traveling parent informing the other parent, in writing, one week before the intended trip.

3. Our child(ren) will not leave the country without being fully covered by appropriate medical insurance and the consent of the other parent, which consent will not be unreasonably withheld.

4. The parent with whom our child(ren) will be traveling will provide the other parent with a travel itinerary and contact number(s) where a message can be left or where he or she can be reached.

SPORADIC CHILDCARE

1. We will each be responsible for making our own child-care arrangements for the temporary alternate care of our child(ren), when such care is needed, with the exception of the conditions set out in the following sections.

2. We will inform the other from time to time who is providing alternate care for our child(ren).

3. We each have the right to communicate with the person who is providing alternate care for our child.

4. If the on-duty parent is going to be absent for a period of .... hours, the other parent will be given the right of first refusal ("right of first care") to care for our child(ren).

CHANGE OF CHILD(REN)'S NAME

Neither of us will change the given name or surname of our child(ren) without the written consent of the other parent.

CHILD(REN)'S TOYS, CLOTHES, AND OTHER BELONGINGS

We recognize that our child(ren) may have particular attachments to certain belongings and will respect the child(ren)'s right to have such belongings transfer with our child(ren) between us when we are in separate homes.

OTHER RELATIONSHIPS EACH CHILD SHARES

1. We will encourage and foster relationships of each child with the other children, family members, and extended family members.

2. If either of us should become incapacitated by reason of illness or misfortune, or if either of us should die, the remaining parent will ensure that our child(ren) will continue to have contact with the extended family of the affected parent.

3. Exceptions:

   ....

   ....

   ....

OTHER ISSUES OR SPECIAL CONCERNS

....

....

....

....

OTHER PROVISIONS FOR DECISION-MAKING

The following special provisions apply to decision-making:

1. If either of us is impaired by drugs, alcohol, fatigue, or any other condition that may affect caregiving, parental responsibility, or judgment in a manner that may affect the well-being of the child(ren), then the other parent may assume sole decision-making authority for the duration of the impairment. The parents agree to consult with a neutral third party as soon as possible to assist in resolving the situation.

2. If either of us subjects the child(ren) to harm through neglect or abuse, then the other parent will assume sole decision-making authority until the situation of neglect or abuse has been dealt with and until such a time as there are reasonable grounds to assume such situations or behavior are not likely to reoccur.

WHEN PROBLEMS ARISE

In the event that we are unable to resolve any particular issue, we agree to resolve the matter through the following:

- Discussion with a friend or family member:

  ....

- Counseling with a neutral third party, therapist, or mediator:

  ....

  ....

- Other:

  ....

  ....

  ....

  ....

Process

1. Either of us may determine if mediation is necessary in order to resolve disagreements and will give written notice that he or she intends to invoke this clause. We agree to meet with the mediator or therapist within ten days or earlier if appointments are available with that professional.

2. The parent who first invokes the clause will be initially responsible for any costs associated with the meeting.

3. The neutral third party will discuss the disagreement with each of us, with a view to working out a mutually satisfactory solution.

4. We agree to empower the mediator to collect such information from third parties as, in the discretion of that professional, will assist in seeking solutions.

5. In the event that the conflict involves an issue that is timely in nature (for example, a medical event other than one that is previously mentioned), we will consider professional advice, obtain a second opinion, if that is necessary, and follow the most prudent course.

COMMUNICATION

Communications will be brief and relate only to issues at hand. We commit to communicating in a courteous manner with the other. We will communicate with each other through the following (check all that apply):

☐ Telephone:

.... : ....

.... : ....

☐ Email:

.... : ....

.... : ....

☐ Online calendar

☐ Texting (for logistical or emergency communication only):

....

☐ "Our Children's Day" notes when going off-duty

☐ Other: ....

RIGHTS

We agree to the following when we are off duty:

1. The right to unimpeded telephone conversations with each child at least .... times a day/week at reasonable times and for a reasonable duration.

2. The right to send mail or email to each child, which the other parent will not open or censor.

3. The right to receive a notice and relevant information as soon as practicable but within twenty-four hours of any event of hospitalization, major illness, or death of each child.

4. The right to receive directly from each child's school copies of each child's report card, attendance records, names of teachers, class schedules, standardized test scores, and any other records customarily made available to parents.

5. The right to receive, directly from each child's physician and other healthcare providers, copies of each child's medical records.

6. The right to be free of derogatory remarks made about the parent or the parent's family by the other parent to or in the presence of the child(ren).

AGREEMENT

We are in agreement with the terms as described earlier. During a legal separation or divorce process, we may discuss the contents of this agreement with our lawyers and obtain independent advice.

.... SIGNATURE	.... DATE
.... SIGNATURE	.... DATE

KEY POINTS TO REMEMBER

- Recognize that parents have different parenting styles.

- Make a clear schedule that serves as your "default" schedule showing when you are on duty.

- Decide about the days or events (holidays, birthdays, school breaks) that will trump the default schedule.

- Make agreements about your children's education, religious or cultural education, extracurricular activities, and social activities.

- Document how you will deal with dating and new relationships.

- Document your agreements regarding your children's medical and mental healthcare.

- Make agreements about when you or your children travel.

- Document how future disagreements will be handled.

- Make a detailed, written, signed agreement in a format such as the worksheet in the previous section. Work with a neutral third party, such as a co-parenting counselor, if needed.

CHAPTER 4

Nesting and Finances

The financial aspect of nesting is an important one that can seem intimidating—but this chapter will take you step-by-step through the process of creating a budget and assessing what you can afford during the nesting period. You will delve into examining the costs of nesting and separation, including maintaining separate living quarters, preserving family resources for the future, planning for taxes, and estimating the potential costs of divorce. You will also learn how to make a realistic budget to maximize the success of your nesting arrangement. The investment you make in organizing and understanding your financial situation will pay off with nesting that runs smoothly.

Honesty and Full Disclosure

It's crucial to talk honestly about money and share all financial information with your spouse or partner. The source of many marital conflicts is money, and if this is the case for you and your partner, it will be important to change the marital dynamic around finances in order to nest. Transparency in everything financial, with a clear understanding and written agreements about who has access to any or all accounts, is the foundation of a solid nesting agreement. If any information is withheld or assets are hidden, the trust between you will break down quickly.

In some states, such as California, "automatic temporary restraining orders" go into effect immediately when people file for divorce. These are temporary legal rules about leaving everything related to money, property, and finances as is. You can no longer make large purchases, change life insurance policies, or sell off significant assets without your spouse's consent (preferably in writing), and so on. Accounts cannot be moved or closed unless you both agree to this.

As your finances are separated during your divorce process, you will need to make informed decisions. For example, the law in California requires full and complete disclosure of everything related to finances and property during a divorce, including several prior years of tax returns and assets that you may consider "separate property." The reason for this is that you need to have a full understanding of your financial picture *before* you start to negotiate a settlement. That's why transparency is essential. (The laws vary in other states.)

Getting Up to Speed with Your Finances

I've worked with many clients who knew nothing about the family finances during their marriage. In many of these cases, the division of labor meant that only one person paid the bills and kept track of spending, investing, and saving. Or one person might have handled day-to-day expenses, while the other handled investments and savings. If you don't understand some or all of your finances, it's time to get some help. An hour or two with a tax preparer or a certified divorce financial analyst (CDFA) to learn and understand your finances will pay off in the long run.

CASE IN POINT

Lisa's husband, Arthur, handled all of their financial matters. She had a credit card and a cash allowance to buy what was needed for the household and was happy with the arrangement.

During their twenty-year marriage, she was happy to let him pay bills and track their bank accounts. At tax time, she simply signed the tax return without really looking at it. She had no interest in money other than being able to purchase food, clothing, and whatever else they needed for the home. She trusted her husband to look after their assets in a responsible way while she cared for their children. When Arthur told her that he wanted a divorce, she was astonished. It was an overwhelming and stressful time for her, and she fell into a major depression.

When Arthur chose a process of divorce that uses lawyers and other family professionals to work out a settlement without going to court, she was shocked to learn that she would need to have access to all of their financial information and understand it, sooner rather than later. This process, which I strongly recommend, that never goes to court and avoids any underlying threat of litigation, is called a collaborative divorce.

Fortunately, a certified public accountant (CPA) was able to go to Lisa's home and educate her about all of the financial papers in her husband's files. Arthur was cooperative in pulling out all of the files, bank statements, tax returns, credit reports, and everything else that Lisa needed to understand their finances.

Why Budgets Are Important

Having a household budget is always important, but especially so if you are nesting. The transparency and clarity that budgeting affords you and your partner can eliminate confusion, suspicion, and conflict.

Some partners have some questions about their spouse's spending—budgeting will bring those issues to light and show you what's really happening. You may realize that you have been spending beyond your means, or that some of your or your partner's discretionary expenses can easily be eliminated.

For most people, budgeting seems like an overwhelming chore, but my experience is that once you begin to do it, it's not difficult, surprisingly revealing, and when you are done, you will appreciate the value of the information.

How to Make a Budget

Making a written budget will be extremely useful in determining whether nesting will make financial sense for you as your finances currently stand, and how to adjust your spending to accommodate nesting if your budget doesn't accommodate it at the moment. You may have never written a budget before, so here are a few suggestions.

The easiest way to put together your budget is to look at your credit card statements and bank statements for the past three months to capture the following:

- Regular fixed monthly expenses like mortgage or rent, utilities (gas, electricity, water), cell phone and Internet, home and auto insurance, car payments, commuting, kids' school tuition (if any)

- Food and grocery costs

- Spending that is discretionary, variable, and under your control, like special clothing, gifts, eating out, and vacations

- Any unexpected or upcoming planned expenses, such as elective surgeries, major home repairs, senior care for aging parents, or car repairs

Another way to do your budget is to write down every penny you spend, every day, for three months. Most people are very surprised by how much they spend and usually see pretty quickly where they can cut back.

The budget template in this chapter provides a framework for you to follow and will prompt you to record expenses that you might otherwise overlook. Once you have identified your hard costs and your expected tax liabilities, you can see what you have each month after taxes. You can also find online budgeting software and apps—but be sure to find one that includes tax consequences, which vary by state.

Sample Budgets

Here are some sample budgets that can give you a quick overview of what's in a budget and how it looks in various scenarios. These budgets reflect federal and California income taxes, which may be different in future years or other states.

SAMPLE BUDGET #1: TWO-INCOME FAMILY WITH A RENTED APARTMENT

This is a sample budget for a two-income family renting an apartment. The off-duty parent stays with either friends or family when not the on-duty parent, so they do not have additional housing expenses. Their health insurance is partially covered with federal subsidies. There are two children.

MONTHLY INCOME	
ABC Company—Spouse #1	$2,500
XYZ Company—Spouse #2	$1,600
TOTAL INCOME (A)	**$4,100**
MONTHLY EXPENSES	
Monthly Family Household Expenses	
Rent Paid	$1,000
Cable/Satellite TV	$100
Internet Service Provider	$50
Trash Removal	$25
Electricity	$100
Water and Sewer	$50
Total Family Household Expenses	**$1,325**
Monthly Transportation Expenses	
Payments (Lease or Financing)	$250
Insurance	$90
Gasoline	$150
Repairs and Maintenance	$50

City Stickers	$50
Public Transportation	$50
Total Transportation Expenses	**$640**
Monthly Child-Related Expenses	
Childcare/Pre-/After-School Care	$150
Clothing for Children	$50
Education Supplies	$10
School Lunch	$50
School-Sponsored Activities	$20
Children Grooming	$30
Doctor	$50
Lessons, Extracurricular Activities	$20
Total Child-Related Expenses	**$380**
Monthly Parents' Personal Expenses	
Cell Phone	$150
Clothing for Adults	$75
Entertainment	$50
Groceries	$700
Gifts	$50
Hair	$60
Laundry	$50
Pet Expenses	$20
Eating Out	$100
Computer/Supplies/Software	$10
Sports and Hobbies	$25
Total Parents' Personal Expenses	**$1,290**

Monthly Health and Medical Expenses	
Health Insurance	$50
Doctor	$50
Orthodontic	$100
Total Health and Medical Expenses	$200
Subtotal Monthly Expenses	**$3,835**
Monthly Savings	
Deductible IRA Contribution	$100
Total Deductible IRA Contribution	$100
TOTAL EXPENSES (B)	**$3,935**
MONTHLY TAXES	
Federal Taxes	($223)
FICA and Medicare	$314
State Taxes (Estimate Only)	$41
Local Wage Tax	$0
TOTAL TAXES (C)	**$132**
TOTAL INCOME (A)	**$4,100**
MINUS TOTAL EXPENSES (B)	**($3,935)**
MINUS TOTAL TAXES (C)	**($132)**
BUDGET NET INCOME	**$33**

SAMPLE BUDGET #2: ONE-INCOME FAMILY WITH A HOME

This is a sample budget for a one-wage-earner family with each parent renting a separate room when off duty. The nonworking parent is looking for work. Health insurance is provided by the employer. There are two children.

MONTHLY INCOME	
Great Company—Spouse #1	$8,300
TOTAL INCOME (A)	**$8,300**
MONTHLY EXPENSES	
Monthly Family Household Expenses	
Rent Paid	$2,300
Cable/Satellite TV	$100
Internet Service Provider	$50
Trash Removal	$25
Electricity	$100
Water and Sewer	$50
Total Family Household Expenses	**$2,625**
Monthly Transportation Expenses	
Payments (Lease or Financing)	$250
Insurance	$180
Gasoline	$300
Repairs and Maintenance	$150
City Parking Permit	$75
Public Transportation	$50
Total Transportation Expenses	**$1,005**
Monthly Child-Related Expenses	
Childcare/Pre-/After-School Care	$300
Clothing for Children	$50
Education Supplies	$10
School Lunch	$50
School-Sponsored Activities	$50

Monthly Child-Related Expenses—*continued*	
Children Grooming	$30
Doctor	$50
Lessons, Extracurricular Activities	$100
Total Child-Related Expenses	$640
Monthly Parents' Personal Expenses	
Cell Phone	$150
Clothing for Adults	$100
Dry Cleaning	$20
Entertainment	$100
Groceries	$700
Gifts	$50
Hair	$60
Laundry	$20
Pet Expenses	$20
Eating Out	$500
Computer/Supplies/Software	$20
Sports and Hobbies	$25
Therapy/Counseling	$150
Total Parents' Personal Expenses	$1,915
Monthly Health and Medical Expenses	
Doctor	$50
Total Health and Medical Expenses	$50
Monthly Expenses—Other	
Room Rental—Spouse #1	$500
Room Rental—Spouse #2	$500

Total Monthly Expenses—Other	$1,000
Subtotal Monthly Expenses	**$7,235**
Monthly Savings	
Deductible IRA Contribution	$100
Total Deductible IRA Contribution	$100
TOTAL EXPENSES (B)	**$7,335**
MONTHLY TAXES	
Federal Taxes	$315
FICA and Medicare	$635
State Taxes (Estimate Only)	$243
Local Wage Tax	$0
TOTAL TAXES (C)	**$1,193**
TOTAL INCOME (A)	$8,300
MINUS TOTAL EXPENSES (B)	($7,335)
MINUS TOTAL TAXES (C)	($1,193)
BUDGET NET INCOME	(-$228)

In this budget, the family is spending beyond their means and will have to cut expenses, at least until the nonworking spouse is able to contribute an income. They decided to cut eating out from $500 to $200, which still left only $72 at the end of the month. They wanted to buy a used car so that they would each have a car while separated, but the budget helped them realize that this would not be possible until a second income was coming in. They also cut entertainment expenses, and the nonworking spouse expanded her job search.

SAMPLE BUDGET #3: TWO-INCOME FAMILY WITH A HOME

This is a sample budget of a family with a family business that pays the family's health insurance. There are two children. The parents have ample income to cover a shared off-duty studio apartment.

MONTHLY INCOME	
Family Business—Spouse #1	$8,000
ABC Company—Spouse #2	$3,000
Family Business Income	$3,750
TOTAL INCOME (A)	$14,750
MONTHLY EXPENSES	
Monthly Mortgage Payments	
5418 Astro Way	$2,300
Total Mortgage Payments	$2,300
Monthly Family Household Expenses	
Rent Paid	$1,500
Homeowners Insurance	$110
Real Estate Taxes, Assessments	$500
Cable/Satellite TV	$100
Internet Service Provider	$100
Land Phone Lines	$105
Repairs and Maintenance	$200
Maid/Cleaning Service	$250
Trash Removal	$25

Electricity	$300
Water and Sewer	$160
Total Family Household Expenses	**$3,350**
Monthly Transportation Expenses	
Insurance	$100
Gasoline	$150
Repairs and Maintenance	$200
License	$30
Tolls	$20
Parking	$25
Total Transportation Expenses	**$525**
Monthly Child-Related Expenses	
Childcare/Pre-/After-School Care	$250
Clothing for Children	$100
School Lunch	$100
School-Sponsored Activities	$30
Children Grooming	$50
Food for Children*	$200
Doctor	$100
Dental	$75
Optical	$50
Lessons, Extracurricular Activities	$150
Total Child-Related Expenses	**$1,105**

*Some parents want to separate children's expenses, which they share, and have each parent be responsible for his or her own food from his or her own separate funds when off duty, or even when on duty.

Monthly Parents' Personal Expenses	
Cell Phone	$150
Clothing for Adults	$150
Dry Cleaning	$50
Club Dues and Membership	$100
Entertainment	$100
Groceries	$700
Gifts	$200
Hair	$150
Manicure, Pedicure	$30
Pet Expenses	$100
Eating Out	$500
Newspapers, Magazines, Books	$50
Travel	$300
Total Parents' Personal Expenses	$2,580
Monthly Health and Medical Expenses	
Health Insurance	$50
Doctor	$200
Dental	$50
Medication	$50
Optical	$75
Total Health and Medical Expenses	$425
Monthly Expenses—Other	
Umbrella Insurance	$65
Total Monthly Expenses—Other	$65
Subtotal Monthly Expenses	**$10,350**

Monthly Savings	
Deductible Simple IRA	$1,500
Total Deductible Simple IRA	$1,500
TOTAL EXPENSES (B)	**$11,850**
MONTHLY TAXES	
Federal Taxes	$1,316
FICA and Medicare	$842
State Taxes (Estimate Only)	$677
Local Wage Tax	$0
TOTAL TAXES (C)	**$2,835**
TOTAL INCOME (A)	$14,750
MINUS TOTAL EXPENSES (B)	($11,850)
MINUS TOTAL TAXES (C)	($2,835)
BUDGET NET INCOME	$65

Budgeting Template

Following is a fairly comprehensive form you can use to create your monthly budget. If you don't need certain categories, just mark 0; if you need to add categories, go ahead.

MONTHLY INCOME	
Salary 1	
Salary 2	
Other wages	
TOTAL INCOME (A)	

MONTHLY EXPENSES	
Housing	
Rent	
1st mortgage average principal	
1st mortgage average interest	
2nd mortgage or line of credit average principal	
2nd mortgage or line of credit average interest	
Real property taxes	
Condo and homeowner association fees	
Homeowners or renters insurance	
Electricity	
Gas, propane	
Water, sewer	
Trash	
Cable TV, satellite TV	
Internet service provider	
Telephone	
Cell phone	
Pest service	
Alarm system	
Maintenance and repair	
Painting and wallpaper	
Furniture and appliance repairs and replacement	
Landscaping	
Pool	
Maid/cleaning service	

Total Housing	
Household	
Groceries	
Groceries for children	
Household supplies	
Liquor, beer, wine	
Cigarettes	
Lottery	
Pets, livestock	
Other supplies	
Laundry	
Dry cleaning	
Total Household	
Employee-Related Expenses	
Mandatory retirement contributions	
Union dues	
Total Employee-Related Expenses	

Childcare	
Childcare—daycare, preschool, sitters, summer camp (job or school related)	
Sitters—not for school or job	
Total Childcare	

Clothing	
Clothes	
Clothes for children	
Total Clothing	

Personal Care	
Manicures, pedicures, skin care	
Hairdresser/barber	
Cosmetics/toiletries	
Total Personal Care	

Children's Expenses	
Tuition	
Room and board	

Extracurricular activities, lessons, supplies	
Entertainment	
Allowance	
Tutors	
School uniforms	
School supplies, books, fees	
School lunch money	
School transportation	
School-sponsored activities	
Summer camps and clubs	
Computer equipment, software, supplies	
Grooming	
Toiletries and related supplies	
Other	
Total Children's Expenses	
Transportation	
Auto insurance	
Gasoline	
Oil changes	
Repairs and maintenance, tires	
Uber/Lyft	
Parking	
Tolls	
Registration, auto club	
Lease or auto loan payments	
Public transportation	

Transportation—*continued*	
Commuting expenses	
Other	
Total Transportation	
Entertainment	
Eating out	
Dues, subscriptions	
Country club dues	
Sports, hobbies	
Health clubs, gym fees	
Movies, plays, sporting events, etc.	
Netflix and other online entertainment	
Newspapers, magazines, books	
Computer equipment, software, supplies	
Travel	
Vacation	
Gifts	
Total Entertainment	
Miscellaneous	
Legal and accounting	
Professional fees	
Income tax preparation	
Financial planning fees	

Bookkeeping	
Bank fees, safe deposit	
Storage	
Charitable contributions	
Religious contributions	
Total Miscellaneous	
Insurance	
Life insurance premiums	
Disability insurance premiums	
Umbrella or other liability insurance premiums	
Long-term care insurance premiums	
Total Insurance	
Savings	
Deferred compensation	
Voluntary 401(k) contributions	
Voluntary IRA contributions	
Savings, investments (nonmandatory)	

Savings—*continued*	
Total Savings	
Health	
Private health, dental, vision insurance premiums—not through an employer	
Unreimbursed medical, such as co-pays, etc. (doctors, hospitals)	
Dental—in excess of the insurance	
Orthodontia	
Vision—in excess of the insurance	
Nonprescription medication, vitamins, supplements—not covered by insurance	
Prescription medication—in excess of or not covered by insurance	
Psychiatrist, psychologist, counseling—not covered by insurance	
Chiropractor, physical therapy, massage—not covered by insurance	
Glasses, contacts—not covered by insurance	
Total Health	
Children's Medical	
Private health, dental, vision insurance premiums—not through an employer	

Unreimbursed medical, such as co-pays, etc. (doctors, hospitals)	
Dental—in excess of the insurance	
Orthodontia	
Vision—in excess of the insurance	
Nonprescription medication, vitamins, supplements—not covered by insurance	
Prescription medications—in excess of or not covered by insurance	
Psychiatrist, psychologist, counseling—not covered by insurance	
Chiropractor, physical therapy, massage—not covered by insurance	
Glasses, contacts—not covered by insurance	
Total Children's Medical	
College	
College tuition	
College room and board	
College books and supplies	
Transportation to/from college	
Total College	

Credit Card Debt	
Credit card debt monthly payments	
Total Credit Card Debt	
TOTAL EXPENSES (B)	
MONTHLY TAXES	
Federal taxes	
FICA and Medicare	
State taxes (estimate only)	
Local income tax	
Other	
TOTAL TAXES (C)	
TOTAL INCOME (A)	
MINUS TOTAL EXPENSES (B)	
MINUS TOTAL TAXES (C)	
BUDGET NET INCOME	

Getting by with Less

After you make a budget, you may find that you need to cut back spending, at least during the nesting period, and perhaps beyond. Many people are surprised by these financial changes, but they are the rule, not the exception. Why? Your income may be reduced due to wages lost from time off work for divorce-related meetings or new childcare responsibilities. You may have to pay legal expenses or counseling costs. Eventually, the income you have may need to support two separate homes if you divorce.

What if you discover that you don't have enough money to cover your fixed costs and basic discretionary expenses? Your choices:

- Increase your income (e.g., a previously nonworking spouse might need to get a job).

- Lower your expenses (e.g., discretionary and recreational spending, such as eating out, private lessons, club memberships, travel, etc.).

- Borrow money (e.g., through a second mortgage, a home equity loan or some other kind of bank lending, or other source like a family member).

- Use your savings or other assets if you have any (this is the time for that rainy-day fund).

Beyond these ideas, out-of-the-box thinking might help you out. For example, one of my clients asked his parents for an advance on his inheritance. Others have taken on a second job when they are off duty. Perhaps older children could babysit or get jobs to help pay some of their own expenses. If you have younger children, you might reduce childcare costs by trading babysitting with other parents. Again, advice from a CPA or CDFA could be very helpful.

DON'T CUT LIFE INSURANCE

One expense that should not be cut is your life insurance (if you have it—if you don't, you should). Your spouse should be the beneficiary of your life insurance policy until the divorce decisions are complete. This is to protect the children in case the owner of the policy dies. It's also a good idea to maintain the life insurance after the divorce with the other parent as beneficiary on behalf of the children.

BEWARE OF CREDIT CARD DEBT

A word of caution if you can't or don't want to cut back your spending: Avoid using credit cards, because the interest rates are exorbitant. If you do continue to use a card for convenience, or because you don't like to carry around a lot of cash, be sure to pay the monthly bill before it becomes overdue, since that way you never pay any interest.

You may be able to set up a line of credit, if necessary, which has a lower interest rate. Withdrawing funds from your retirement accounts or 529 education accounts can have serious tax penalties, up to 50 percent if you are not 59.5 years old. This should be a last resort.

Determining Your Nesting Housing Situation Using Your Budget

After you've drafted your existing budget and have a handle on your discretionary assets and spending (over which you have some control), then you will see what money could be used for a room or apartment for your off-duty time. You will see whether you and your spouse can each have an off-duty living space, or whether you may be able to share one space.

Housing prices have generally increased over the past decade, but there are exceptions in certain neighborhoods and specific houses, so take the time to search extensively. Be sure to estimate what other costs you will need to pay as well, including utilities, possibly Internet, and any furnishings that you may need to rent or purchase. Some people take some furnishings from the family home or find used furniture online, or borrow from friends and family. Others will need to add the extra expense of travel if your off-duty apartment is some distance away, where rents are lower.

If you can't afford an off-site residence, even with the cut-backs that you can make, you'll need to brainstorm other solutions, as described in Chapter 2. You might be able to stay with friends or family, for example, or find a way to section a part of your home as the off-duty site. In the ABC TV sitcom *Splitting Up Together*, the parents made the garage into a decent off-duty living space, which they shared.

Incorporating Your Budget Into Your Nesting Agreement

Now it's time to decide what financial changes you need to make during nesting and how income is shared during the nesting period—and update your budget with that information. This updated budget will go into your nesting agreement, which you'll formalize in the next chapter.

Make sure that this nesting budget includes the expenses of the off-duty residence, as well as setting aside some money for taxes and future divorce-related expenses, if possible. The budgeting plan needs detailed financial agreements to include information such as which one of you pays which bills. It should spell out how the money will be spent in the family home and whether you will use credit cards or savings.

NESTING BANK ACCOUNTS

Some couples set up a nesting bank account that will cover joint expenses during this time period. You will need to agree on how much to deposit or what percentage of each of your incomes will go into this account. For example, some of my clients agree to each put in 50 percent of their income, regardless of their salaries. Others agree to each put in a specific dollar amount. If there is just one breadwinner, you'll need to decide how much can go into the nesting account.

I also suggest that you and your spouse set a maximum dollar amount (perhaps $50 or $100) that you can spend from the nesting account without necessarily asking permission from your spouse. This type of expense is generally discretionary and could be something such as new electronics or special occasion clothing for your children.

You may decide to put some payments on auto pay programs that are available in most banks, or clarify who is responsible for which bills. You might also choose to have your bank and/or credit card companies alert each of you whenever a transaction takes place. This transparency will build trust.

KEEPING MONEY SEPARATE

You may decide to also have separate bank accounts or credit cards to pay for your own personal, discretionary spending, such as dating or entertainment. Even if you each control your separate accounts or credit cards, you still need to share information and agree about how much you are keeping separate for now. This is part of the full disclosure required by law in most states.

DEALING WITH TAXES AND CREDIT SCORES

If your credit reports show that you need to do any work to improve your credit score, do that before you separate or divorce. The reason is that when you are looking for a lease, an insurance quote, or a new credit card, all those people will check your credit score and report.

While you're legally married and have joint debt in both your names, your credit score will be affected if one of you doesn't stay current on payments. Your spouse's credit score doesn't affect you, however, unless you try to take out more debt with that person.

You might have joint debt after your divorce, moreover, so you'll need to trust (or at least pay attention) that the debt is paid according to the terms required by the creditor. Any loan or credit card debt taken before the date of separation in most community property states is legally considered joint debt.

A final note: In some states, you're still technically married while you're nesting. Therefore, in some states, the income and expenses are still considered "joint," so check with a local CPA about this if you have a question.

CASE IN POINT

Jack and Allie decided to open a new nesting bank account and nesting credit card from which all nesting-related expenses and children's expenses were paid. They initially funded it by each depositing 40 percent of their separate paychecks. They agreed to charge all the children's expenses on a dedicated credit card so that they could track the spending. They were also determined to pay the credit card off every month to avoid the exorbitant interest charges. After several months, they reviewed their expenses and increased their deposits to 50 percent of their paychecks.

Review Your Financial Situation Periodically

It's a good idea to sit down once a month and review all the monthly statements and bills together. If possible, meet in a quiet place away from your children. A coffee shop would be one such place or at a picnic table in a sparsely populated location. If you are not comfortable meeting in person, perhaps a neutral third person, whom you both trust, can join you. (Of course, you should review your budget together immediately if there's been any significant change in circumstances, such as a job loss or rising housing costs.) During your budget check-ins, you two can do the following:

- Consider how to fund any new upcoming expenses.

- Discuss what worked and what didn't work financially in the past month for each of you.

- Resolve conflict—for example, if one of you didn't adhere to your spending agreement or if someone didn't pay a bill that needed to be paid.

- Look back at the last month's spending from the nesting account or credit card to see where the money is going and if there were unusual, new, or extraordinary expenses. Examples of these expenses might be counseling for your child or summer camp fees.

- Evaluate whether the money deposited in your nesting account is sufficient to keep your nesting stable, or whether you need to increase funding, or cut back or eliminate some expenditures.

Working together on financial matters might be awkward at first, but it will build trust between you and support successful nesting.

Future Expenses

Other considerations in the financial realm include retirement planning, estate planning, future educational costs, and weddings, etc. If you haven't yet begun saving money for these items, it will probably be difficult to start right now. If you have already begun to save for retirement or for your children's education, try to at least preserve those funds. Some of these savings or contributions might have to be stopped for a while to pay for the divorce or nesting. Consult professionals to help you make decisions that have important implications for both your and your children's future.

KEY POINTS TO REMEMBER

- Successful nesting requires financial honesty and total transparency.

- Full and complete disclosure of all income and debt is required by law.

- If you or your spouse need help to understand your finances, consult your CPA.

- Develop your complete budget, including all income and expenses now and when you begin nesting.

- Use the numbers to see what you can afford, as well as how income and expenses will be shared.

CHAPTER 5

Creating a Nesting Agreement That Works

In this chapter, you will learn about how to draft a nesting agreement that is customized for your family and increases the ease and success of your nesting period. We will explore the various issues you will want to include in your nesting agreement, as well as ways to make this time period calm and conflict-free. You'll use the co-parenting plan you made in Chapter 3 and the budget you made in Chapter 4 as foundations for this agreement.

Using Your Co-Parenting Plan As a Foundation for Nesting

The co-parenting plan that you agreed upon in Chapter 3 and the budget you created in Chapter 4 will make your transition into nesting so much easier. The breadth of topics you've covered means that you're ready to handle most of what will come up on a daily basis. When you decide to nest, you need specific agreements about how nesting will work. The nesting agreement is a written, signed agreement that the two of you make, but it is not a legal document, nor is it enforceable by the court. This document addresses the logistics of nesting. The agreements specifically address how you will be parenting and sharing the home while nesting. You can include any additional issues that you believe will help your specific or unique needs.

Later, when you separate or divorce, the legal process includes a *parenting plan*. At a minimum, it describes the amount of time the children will spend with each parent. It does not necessarily address specific *parenting* agreements or practices, although many people choose to add those as well. In fact, you may choose to include the co-parenting plan that you created in Chapter 3, or you might modify it when nesting ends.

Little Details Can Make a Big Difference

Many factors will affect how well nesting works for your family. Thinking of as many as possible ahead of time will help you avoid conflict and confusion. Cleanliness is at the top of the list of common complaints. When the on-duty parent rotates out of the home (or perhaps a shared off-site apartment) and leaves behind dishes in the sink, piles of laundry, unchanged bed linens, or a full garbage can, the incoming parent will probably not be thrilled. Of course, larger issues such as how to change over from on duty to off duty are also important. As you discuss the specifics of nesting, consider these questions:

- **How will you change from on duty to off duty?** It is usually best when parents have as little overlap as possible, as this is a possible point of tension for your children and you. Therefore, if the transition happens while your children are at school, for example, it will go more easily. (That means that the on-duty parent drops your children off at school and then goes off duty.) The other parent will go on duty to pick them up.

- **How will you handle grocery shopping?** Your plan should include specifically what you expect to find in the fridge and pantry when you come on duty. Does this seem too small an issue to detail? Not if it prevents an argument or feelings of resentment. If you live in an area with a reasonably priced grocery-delivery service, consider using that regularly to minimize stress on all parties.

- **Are visits to the family home permitted?** Some parents want to include agreements about boundary issues, such as whether or under what conditions the off-duty parent (and her or his extended family, such as grandparents, aunts, and uncles) may come into the home during the parent's off-duty time. Coming into the home when you are off duty unannounced or without prior agreement can upset your co-parent and your children.

- **How will you divide up chores and housekeeping?** Who will take out the trash, clean the bathrooms, and mow the lawn—and when? Should the thermostat be at any particular temperature?

- **How will you handle big-picture maintenance and repairs?** Who will handle larger issues, like getting a new roof? How will it be paid for?

- **Will you establish rules about personal property?** Nesting requires an agreement that neither of you will move or remove personal possessions or important documents without prior agreement. Any common property, such as photo albums, antiques, and important paperwork, should be left in the home. If you move personal possessions or household goods (e.g., pots and pans) to your off-site location, be sure to discuss what you will be taking and come to agreement about what stays and what can go.

Each of you should have a private space in the home for personal items that won't be touched by your spouse. This includes computers, for example. Nesting will probably fail if one of you searches the other's computers, mail, or private papers. It will be experienced as disrespectful and an intrusive violation of privacy.

CASE IN POINT

Justin and Jess had three children, one of whom, Meghan, had severe anorexia. Prior to their separation, Meghan had been hospitalized. Until the decision to nest, Jess had been the primary parent, supervising Meghan's treatment, while Justin was the breadwinner. Now Justin would need to be brought up to speed about their daughter's treatment plan. Their nesting agreement included the specific meal and eating plans prescribed by the child's doctor, as well as regular therapy and visits to the pediatrician for weight checks.

Both parents agreed to keep all of these appointments and to work with their treating professionals to help their daughter recover. They also agreed to keep a daily log, online, so that both parents could monitor Meghan's weight and eating. These agreements were documented in their nesting agreement.

Be Patient with Each Other

Nesting and separation cause a redefining of parenting roles to that of single parents, and that comes with a learning curve and new responsibilities. Co-parenting is not easy, even if your separation was not acrimonious. It may be difficult to separate your feelings about your co-parent from your desire to co-parent effectively. It can help to think of it as a completely new relationship: a co-parenting relationship, not a "couple" relationship. Ideally, as single parents, you'll work cooperatively together to co-parent and help your children feel secure. How much you cooperate and communicate depends on where you land on the co-parenting continuum.

HELP EACH OTHER OUT

Give yourself and each other some time to adjust to the new reality and new roles. Before you separated, you probably had an informal division of labor, as well as different parenting styles. One of you may have been the breadwinner, perhaps in charge of religious studies, watering the yard and taking out the trash, or paying the bills. The other may have been in charge of school projects, transportation to and from sports practices, shopping for school supplies, clothing, and cooking meals. You divided the tasks to make things run smoothly, and you probably never talked explicitly about this division of labor.

How you parented probably differed also. One of you may have been more organized, more nurturing, more playful, while the other may have been more structured, the disciplinarian, the rule setter. Over time, one of you may have become more and more strict in order to compensate for the other parent's perceived lax, indulgent, or inconsistent parenting. In response, the more lenient parent may have become even more lenient or indulgent to make up for the other parent's meticulous rule following. This dynamic—trying to compensate for what you believe is your co-parent's poor parenting—is not good for your relationship, nor is it good for your children. It may have even contributed to the end of your relationship. In fact, what your children need from both of you is a balance of fun, love, and support, as well as guidance, values, limits, and follow-through with rules.

You'll need to learn to do much of what your co-parent used to do, while at the same time developing your own ways of doing those things. Learning new tasks may be extra difficult because your children may be missing their other parent and the way things were before the separation. As one child said to her dad as he boiled hot dogs one night, "That's not the way Mom does it. I like hers better. She makes us good dinners, and I wish she were here." Dad's appropriate response was "I know it's different now, and I am just figuring out how you like your hot dogs. Would you like to cook with me? We can figure it out together."

When you are on duty you'll be in charge of shopping, laundry, cooking, homework, and preparing your children for school, although you may not have done all of these things in the past. You may need to manage home repairs, pay the bills, or take out the trash, even if that was not your role before. My advice is to help each other learn the tasks that are new—give each other a hand so you can both be successful. If that's not possible, at least try to be patient with each other as you learn. You should both expect a learning curve, but trust that you will each rise to the occasion.

CASE IN POINT

When Jack and Allie, whom you met earlier in this book, first separated, Allie was not fully prepared to deal with house crises as they came up. Within the first few weeks, she called Jack in a panic because ants had invaded the kitchen. Jack dropped everything to come over and spray the ants and call an exterminator.

Jack then showed Allie more about the house maintenance and repairs that he had previously done. This experience helped Allie to see how dependent she was on Jack for certain things and how hard it was for her to let him go. While they didn't discuss this particular dynamic together, they did deal with it separately. Allie talked about it with her therapist, who helped her accept and adjust to the separation. Jack began to set some appropriate boundaries with Allie, using a kind and thoughtful approach that encouraged her independence.

IF YOU'RE STRUGGLING TO ACCEPT SINGLE PARENTHOOD

You may feel resentful about having to learn to be a single parent, especially if you didn't want the separation or divorce and/or you now need to get a job. If you were a full-time parent and you will now be working, you are also grieving the loss of parenting responsibilities. If that's the case, consider therapy to talk through your feelings. In the meantime, you might think about how some single parents put a positive spin on being a single parent by focusing on some positive aspects: They have full authority, they don't get into arguments about who does what, and they get frequent breaks when they go off duty.

Making Nesting Successful via Trust

The single most important way to ensure your nesting will be successful is to cultivate trust. The challenge is that many marriages end because trust has been eroded or erased. There may have been betrayals, losses, or a pattern of frequent arguments. You might believe that the person you married has changed in some significant way, or your partner might feel that about you. No matter why you or your partner now feel a loss of trust, you have to deal with it in order to nest.

Fortunately, there is a way to rebuild the kind of trust you need to nest, and it's easier than you might think. What you need to do is practice making simple agreements together and adhering to them. If you and your partner come to these agreements with a genuine spirit of compromise and commitment, it will be easier for both of you to keep up your end of the bargain. These agreements must be written and signed by both of you. This is to eliminate (or at least reduce) misunderstandings about what the agreements are.

It's important to be sure that your agreements are made in the right frame of mind. In the past, you (or your spouse) may have agreed to something because you caved in or were too exhausted or frustrated to argue—you just wanted to move on. Those agreements are not really agreements at all. In my work with clients, I often have to stop people and ask them about this directly. "Is this something you can really accept and honor, or are you just wanting to end the conversation?" I have also seen many examples of agreements that one person thought was made, but the other swears up and down that he or she had not actually agreed. If you don't agree with something, then don't say you do. You can say, "I will think about it," or "That doesn't work for me."

Agreements made in the wrong frame of mind are extremely difficult to honor. Broken agreements break down trust and will likely lead to the failure of the nesting, so do your best to make your agreements genuine and then honor them. In addition, you should not assume that you have an agreement unless it is specific, documented, and signed.

CASE IN POINT

Hillary and Jared had discussed their expectations in detail. In their nesting agreement, they included their mutual expectations regarding the condition of the home (and their shared studio apartment) when the on-duty parent comes in. Because it was a small studio, Hillary asked Jared to vacuum each time he left to go on duty. She was annoyed to find crumbs on the carpet when she came in. Jared didn't care whether Hillary vacuumed when she left the studio, but he was triggered when he saw her toiletries scattered in the bathroom. He asked her to be sure that her toiletries were packed into a small basket when she left. Their agreements honored each of their requests, and keeping those agreements built trust.

George and Kathy hadn't been so diligent in their agreement. Once, he was frustrated when he found there wasn't any milk in the refrigerator. He'd been sleeping at his office and eating a lot of fast food during his off-duty time and counted on Kathy to keep the refrigerator stocked. They had not included their expectations in their nesting agreement, so they were not on the same page. Fortunately, when they discussed this, George was able to make a short list of the items he wanted to find in the fridge when he came on duty. Kathy understood how hard it was for him to eat fast food so often and agreed to his request. This also helped rebuild the trust they needed to nest successfully.

Focus On What Matters to Each of You

Despite your best efforts, disagreements between you and your ex are bound to arise now and then as you are nesting. The key to dealing with them is to keep what's best for the children at the forefront of your mind and to identify any underlying emotions or fears that lie behind the disagreement. Try to talk calmly about why you disagree and why it matters to you. It may help your partner understand if you can name and talk about your feelings too. This may also offer a solution to the problem at hand.

CASE IN POINT

Barb and Olivia, who were introduced earlier in the book, were discussing how they would structure the on-duty/off-duty schedule. Barb wanted to have the changeover occur on Saturday evenings so each parent would have one weekend day with their young twin boys, and one day off duty. She couldn't bear the idea of not seeing their children over an entire weekend. Beyond that, Barb also wasn't confident that Olivia would prepare their children for their school week and would rather the kids were with her (Barb) so she could make sure they got enough sleep and had finished all their homework.

However, Olivia wanted the changeover to occur on Monday so that she would have an entire weekend with their adopted twins during her on-duty time. She liked to go camping with their children and felt that Barb's concerns about their children's sleep and schoolwork were unfounded.

This kind of disagreement is quite typical in separating families and conveys the lack of trust between the parents. In this situation, Barb did not yet fully trust Olivia because of her affair. I was able to help each of the parents understand the other's perspective by encouraging them to articulate what underlay their positions. Barb was still grieving about Olivia's affair, and she admitted that a part of her wanted to hurt or punish Olivia. Olivia admitted that she had long felt that Barb did not respect her parenting and wanted to prove to her that she was a committed parent, despite her affair. Once they were able to communicate their understanding to each other, they could begin to brainstorm some possible solutions.

Barb understood that their children and Olivia loved their camping weekends, and thinking about their children, she didn't want to interfere with that. Olivia was able to reassure Barb about her concerns and asked Barb for some help getting up to speed since she had not been very involved with their children's schoolwork, something that she wanted very much to change. She acknowledged that in fact she had been somewhat less involved as a parent and really wanted to change that. She also agreed that when she didn't take the children camping, she would offer Barb an opportunity to see them at some point over the weekends that she was on duty.

Create Your Personalized Nesting Agreement

The following template addresses the logistics of nesting. The agreements specifically address how you will be sharing the home while nesting. You can include any additional issues that you believe will help your specific or unique needs. Be sure to make realistic agreements, and remember that keeping your agreements will help rebuild trust. One way to start your nesting agreement is to copy the mission statement from your parenting plan. This provides the reference point for all of the many decisions you will consider in your plan. It is a positive, hopeful, and sincere forecasting of how you will work as co-parents.

MISSION STATEMENT AND GOALS FOR NESTING

....

....

....

AGREEMENTS

Schedule
Schedule will be reviewed and revised as needed. It is currently:

....

....

Transitioning from On Duty to Off
- We will avoid overlap when possible
- Changeover occurs after drop-off at school
- Transition will occur in this way:

....

....

Expectations about the Condition of the Home at the Time of Transition
- Dishes clean and put away
- Laundry finished and put away
- Bed and bath linens clean
- Litter box cleaned
- Garbage/compost cans emptied

- Nothing removed from the home without prior agreement
- What we expect to find in the fridge or pantry:

....

....

COMMUNICATION

We will have regular check-ins, when and by what means:

- Meet weekly at coffee shop to review schedule and other concerns
- Leave an Our Children's Day memo at home on kitchen counter
- Send a text message if running more than ten minutes late
- Use email for substantive issues, and texts for logistics
- No posting about each other, our social life, or the kids on social media
- We will work together to solve problems if they occur while we nest, and if we disagree we will:

....

....

HOME MAINTENANCE, REPAIRS, AND FINANCES

- Who will pay the bills: ....
- How repairs and maintenance are handled (who is responsible):

....

....

- Who will water the houseplants: ....
- Kids' allowance (who gives it and how much): ....

....

....

- Kids' expected chores: ....
  ....
- We will not purchase anything over $.......................... without
  the consent of the other parent

PERSONAL PRIVACY

- Respect each other's personal possessions, computers, mail,
  private papers
- No trash-talking the other parent
- No questioning the kids about the other parent, using them
  as confidantes, spies, or messengers

SPECIFIC ISSUES OF SPECIAL CONCERN

1. Special needs of the children:
   ....
   ....

2. Necessary attention to medication or dietary needs of children:
   ....
   ....

3. Where we will leave the mail:
   ....

4. Agreement that no dates brought to the family home:
   ....

5. Agreement that we will only date when off duty:
   ....

6. Agreement on under what conditions the off-duty parent
   may come into the home: ....
   ....

7. Agreement on the use of drugs and alcohol when on duty:
   ....
   ....

ENDING NESTING

How much notice to give if one of us wants to end the nesting:

....

....

The Ready-to-Nest Pledge

Are you now ready to nest? If so, you can now both sign this ready-to-nest pledge to ensure your nesting will be safe, rewarding, and healing for you and your children.

- I will work with my co-parent to create a nesting agreement tailored to the needs of our children and family.

- I will process my own emotions separately from nesting and prioritize the needs of my children.

- I will make every effort to use the recommended guidelines to improve communication with my spouse.

- I am satisfied with the mission and agreements we have documented in our nesting agreement and commit to keeping that to which I have agreed.

- I will not use our children as messengers or confidantes.

- I will be reliable about showing up on time and will leave the home in good condition when I go off duty.

KEY POINTS TO REMEMBER

The nesting agreement consists of the following:

- The on-duty/off-duty schedule and the related logistics.

- Keeping the children out of the middle, not using them as confidantes, messengers, or spies.

- The condition in which you will each care for the home and how you will leave the home when you go off duty.

- Agreements about dating and new relationships.

- Commitments around privacy, private space, computers, mail, and social media.

- Respecting and not using or removing personal property and papers.

- How to deal with damage to the home or personal property.

- How bills and other expenses will be paid.

- How decisions will be made and what to do if you don't agree.

- When, what, how, and how much you will communicate with each other.

- Agreements that either of you can ask to reassess how the plan is working and change it by agreement only.

- Agreements about how nesting will be ended.

Part Two

Implementing Your Nesting Plan

THE FOLLOWING CHAPTERS will help you implement the co-parenting plan and nesting agreement that you created in Part 1. The first step will be to share the news with your children and close friends and family members. Since many people have not heard of nesting, you will need to be able to explain your plan and ask for their support. In Chapter 7, you will learn about what information needs to be shared between you and your co-parent when you are nesting and how to do it in a way that benefits your kids.

CHAPTER 6

Talking to Your Kids (and Others) about Nesting

Sharing the news about nesting with your children, family, and friends should be your priority after you finalize your nesting agreement. Although many parents have chosen to nest over the years, the nesting process is still not widely known or understood. In this chapter, we'll consider how and when to talk to your children and others about your nesting agreement and any changes that may subsequently arise, such as the decision to end the nesting, to reconcile, to divorce, or to sell the home.

This chapter will also prepare you for feedback you may receive, most of which is probably unwanted. While your friends and family may have well-intentioned advice and divorce horror stories that they feel compelled to share with you, try not to get bogged down in other people's lives and instead focus on the agreements and plans you and your partner have made. Reassure loved ones that you have trusted guidance or professionals who are on board to help you. You can also let your support network know that you will ask when you would like advice.

Use Reassuring Language

The words you use shape the way you and others think. The common language around divorce tends to seed conflict, rather than cooperation. Following are some suggestions of words you might use when talking to your children and others about your nesting and divorce. These wording changes establish a non-adversarial tone, which is reassuring to your children, who might have heard frightening divorce stories from their friends. Using these terms also helps set a certain expectation of other adults, showing them the words you'll be using with the children so they can use them as well.

- **"Shared/sharing parenting time":** Try to avoid using "custody," which is also a term used to describe the detention of suspects in a legal sense. This is not child-friendly. Likewise, sometimes we talk of the parent who "gets visitation." This doesn't value the parental responsibility of both parents, their love for their children, nor the attachment that children need to have to both parents. My suggestion is to use the term "sharing parenting time" with your children.

- **Use kid-focused terminology:** You'll foster more positive connections when you look at the needs of your children and phrase things according to their viewpoint. My divorcing clients often say, "It's my day with the kids," but it's more child focused to say, "It's your time with Mom this week." Here's another phrase you can tweak to focus on the children: "Dad's house" should be "home with Dad." This is child-centered language.

- **"One family":** Instead of "broken home," I prefer "one family under two roofs." "Broken home" implies that there are permanent damages and failure, but children can and do adjust to the emergence of a restructured family and thrive after a divorce.

These terms might take some getting used to, but they'll help assure your children that their needs are most important. "We are still one family under two roofs" is very comforting to children.

Talk First with Your Children

Once you and your spouse have made your decision to nest, it will be important to talk first with your children. You want them to hear the news from you in a loving way. In the 1950s, when my parents divorced, children usually learned of their parents' divorce when they came home from school to discover that one parent was gone. Even today, many parents avoid talking to their children before the changes start to unfold. Yet they can often find out via another channel—they might overhear other adults talking about your divorce, or be asked about it by school friends who have heard rumors from their parents—which is understandably upsetting.

WHAT TO SAY AND HOW TO SAY IT

For these reasons, the first step is to plan with your spouse how and when you will talk to your children. Here are some tips:

- **Plan ahead:** You and your spouse should meet ahead of time to draft what you would like to say to your children. You don't need to write out a whole script, but decide who is going to start the conversation and agree on the points you would like to make.

- **Gather everyone at once:** It is important to have all of your children together when they hear the news. If one sibling hears earlier than the others, he or she will either have to carry the burden of the secret or the burden of informing his or her siblings without the benefit of your guidance.

- **Schedule the talk wisely:** Scheduling the exact day and time of the talk is also important. Avoid a time you'd be rushed (in the morning of a school day) or trying to do it at or near bedtime (when everyone is tired). It shouldn't be near or on a holiday or your child's birthday. Choose a weekend morning, perhaps, when you'll be able to spend some time with your children after you've had the conversation. This reassures them that you will each still be parenting them. In addition, children may have somewhat delayed emotional reactions or new questions. Spending some time together after the talk gives them time to process the news.

- **Explain what nesting is:** "We have decided to do something called 'nesting' or 'birdnesting.' Like birds who fly in and out of the nest to care for their babies, we will take turns being here with you every four days. What will change is that either Mom or Dad will be here with you at the house, but we won't be here at the same time. We will put a calendar on the fridge so you always know who is going to be here at home with you. We aren't sure about a lot of other things yet, but as soon as we figure them out, we will tell you."

- **Make your messages age-appropriate:** Younger children and older children will have different ways of understanding and reacting to your news. So, make sure that your announcement is age-appropriate. Each child will undoubtedly have her or his own reactions, questions, and emotions, so just do your best to respond in a way that matches the child's developmental stage. If you have a four-year-old and a twelve-year-old, for example, you might say that "Mommy and Daddy will be taking turns being home with you. Sometimes Mommy will be here, and sometimes Daddy. You will always have Mommy or Daddy here with you." One family showed their toddler by using the child's dollhouse, moving grown-up figures in and out. Your twelve-year-old is able to understand much more, and you will be the best judge of what he or she can understand. This will be the first of many conversations, so trust that your older children will understand after more discussion.

- **Avoid blaming the other parent:** Children are usually black-and-white thinkers and don't have an understanding of adult relationships. They will often try to decide which of you is at fault and which of you needs their loyalty or seems to be the most fragile. They will often believe that one of you needs their emotional support and that one of you is "bad" and to blame for the divorce. This isn't healthy for your children because they need you both, and you will both need to continue to love and parent them. It will be up to you two to craft a non-blaming narrative, even if something traumatic has led to the separation, such as one of you having an affair.

While I understand how angry, resentful, or frustrated you may feel, I can tell you that your children do *not need to know* whom you feel is responsible for the breakup. It isn't healthy for them, and it could cause years of suffering as they try to figure it out. Say something like "We have decided that our marriage cannot make us happy," or "We feel we have grown apart and don't want to live together anymore," or perhaps "We have decided we need to make some changes." Notice that these introductory sentences all start with "we." That is done intentionally to show that you've made a joint decision.

- **Set expectations:** You should tell your children what will change and what will stay the same. Note that you cannot make promises about that of which you are not yet certain. It might look like this: "You will still go to your school and sleep on your pillow. You will still have your soccer team practices. We will still have Christmas with your cousins. Many other things will stay the same for now. And some things will change."

- **Answer questions honestly:** Your children may ask you whether they'll have to move or if you are going to get divorced. If you haven't made those decisions, simply let them know that you still have a lot of things to think about. If you are both certain about your answers, then go ahead and answer them as honestly as you can. For example: "We will definitely be here in the house for the rest of the school year, and then we will have to sell our house next summer so that we can each find a place to live separately later, when we stop nesting. We are going to try to stay in this neighborhood so you can go to the same school. But we aren't yet sure we'll be able to do that. We will do our best and keep you posted."

- **Reassure, reassure, reassure:** Another extremely important part of your conversation is reassurance. More than the information, your children need to know that you both love them, that you will both be their parents forever, that grownups never divorce their children, and so on. You can explain, "Sometimes parents fall out of love, but they never stop loving their children. And we won't ever stop loving you."

- **Make sure they know they're not to blame:** The children will also need to understand, very clearly, that they did not cause the divorce. And they need to understand that there is nothing they can do to change the outcome. For example: "Sometimes kids think that their parents divorce because a child is 'bad.' This is definitely not true, and our decision is just about us not being happy together. When we got married, we didn't think this would ever happen, and we are sad about it. But you did nothing to cause this, and there is nothing you can do to change it. These are grown-up problems, and we both want you to keep on being the wonderful kids that you are. You don't need to worry about us or take care of us."

- **Don't hide your emotions:** Parents often ask me "What if I break down and cry when we talk to the kids?" It would be fine if you got teary, and many parents do. You don't need to be stoic. It models something important to your children: that everyone will have feelings, all feelings are okay, and that things will get better. You can acknowledge it with words like, "Yes, it's sad, and we'll all have a lot of feelings about this change. It's okay to have feelings, and we want you to talk to us about your feelings and your questions. Even if you see Mom or Dad looking upset or even crying, remember that all feelings are okay, and we both have a lot of support and help from other grown-ups. Even if we're upset, we know it will all be okay in the end. We will all need time to get used to these changes, but things will be okay." What will definitely frighten your children is if you fall apart, get hysterical, or start to argue with your spouse. Preparing ahead of time will help you manage your emotions so this doesn't happen.

FOLLOW UP

You may or may not have an idea of what to expect from your children when you tell them about the changes that are coming. And what you expect may or may not be what transpires. You might predict that one child will shut down with no response, and instead that child has an extreme emotional reaction. Some children might be shocked, and other intuitive children may not be surprised at all.

Any and all reactions are fine, so allow your children to have their own responses. Some children need time to process the news, and others may have immediate reactions and questions. In either case, reassure your children that they can talk more about the nesting and the separation whenever they feel like it.

If your children don't say much over the next few days, you could ask, "So, how are you doing about this change to nesting?" While you don't need to drag their feelings out forcibly, you should continue to check in periodically and let them know that it's okay to talk about them.

WHAT YOUR KIDS WISH YOU KNEW

This list, developed by and used with permission of Isolina Ricci, PhD (and excerpted from "Divorce from the Kids' Point of View," *NCFR Report*, December 2007), captures what I've often heard from children in my practice. Think of these statements as you prepare and talk to your children:

1. We need to know you love us, will protect us, and won't leave us.
2. Help us get organized for your going back and forth. Be patient.
3. Listen to our questions and opinions even if you don't agree.

4. Accept that we need a lot of time to adjust, even if we don't show it.
5. Keep your conflicts and dislike of each other out of sight and earshot.
6. Keep us out of the middle of your problems. We are just kids.
7. Don't ask us to spy, pass messages, or hear you put down the other parent.
8. Give us a chance to talk with other kids who are also going through this.
9. Help us express our feelings and learn how to manage them.
10. Give us space and time to grieve the loss of our old life at our own pace.
11. Confide in people your own age. We are not your substitute spouse.
12. Tell us we aren't at fault for your problems. We can't fix them either.
13. Show us it's OK to love and want to be with both of you.

If your children seem to be struggling with the news or the changes, consider some counseling for them. A therapist who specializes in working with children, or a group for kids going through divorce would offer them support.

Talking with Extended Family and Friends

Now that you have shared the news with your children, you'll need to share it with others, especially those who will be supporting your children and family over the next period of time. These include your immediate and extended family, your children's teachers and caregivers, and close family, friends, and neighbors.

CASE IN POINT

Hillary and Jared printed up a small card that they simply handed to family and friends when they spoke with them. They also emailed it out jointly to friends outside the area. They wrote the following:

To our family and dear friends: We have decided to sepa-rate and have talked with our children about our decision. We are going to "nest" for some time before we make fur-ther changes and would like to tell you a little bit about what we will be doing.

While our children stay in our home, we will be alter-nating being in the home with them. When we are off duty, each of us will be rotating in and out of a rented studio apartment nearby. We believe that this period of nesting will help our kids feel safe, secure, and stable while we all get used to the changes and make some other decisions.

We ask for your support: Please don't feel that you need to take sides. Our relationship with you is important to both of us and we don't want you to choose sides. Also, please know that we have professional guidance as we go through this process. More than your advice, we would like your emotional support (and maybe sometimes help with the kids).

Jared and Hillary

It's really helpful to have the support of extended family and friends, but they may not know what nesting is or may not fully embrace the concept. Here's how to share your news with these people.

1. **Explain how your nesting agreement will work, why you have chosen to nest, and how it will help your children**

and family. Use the key points from Chapter 1 as your foundation.

2. **Ask for what you need in the way of specific support.** If you want to ask them to continue their current childcare arrangement, for example, ask if that's all right.

3. **Reassure them as you reassured your children.** For example, you might tell your in-laws and your parents that grandparents are always welcome in the home no matter which parent is on duty (if that is indeed the case—if not, share another piece of reassuring news).

4. **Ask people not to "take sides."** Using non-blaming and non-adversarial language helps set an appropriate tone.

5. **Outline your requests about how they share your news with third parties.** Parents often want to control what news is shared and not shared and with whom, and this includes on social media channels. Discuss, clarify, and agree on the desired message you and your partner would like to give people, and then tell them. The more unified your message, the less conflict others will perceive, and the more likely others will support your decisions.

Ideally, talking to most of your family and friends will be similar to your conversation with your children. You each probably have special confidantes with whom you might share deeper feelings about the decision to separate. Perhaps you have a counselor or therapist you can talk to. Just be aware that rumors spread quickly, and while you cannot control others' reactions to the news, you can control your own public message.

CASE IN POINT

When Emma started to tell her parents that she had decided to leave her husband, Brad, the first thing her father said was, "You'd better lawyer up right away." But Emma and Brad had already decided that their separation would not be adversarial, despite Emma's grief and anger about his affair. In fact, Emma told Brad that if he would make some changes, including going to therapy and giving up his girlfriend, that she would reconsider the decision to divorce. They agreed that they were going to nest for a while to give them the time to think about next steps. They were very concerned about how their son William would adjust to a major change in the family.

Emma asked her father to back off, hear her out, and support the decisions she and Brad had made about their nesting and next steps. "What I really need right now is just emotional support," she explained. "Please don't feel you have to take sides. I know you are just looking out for my interests, and I'm grateful...but I am getting professional help for my financial and legal options."

KEY POINTS TO REMEMBER

- Work together to prepare a non-blaming message using thoughtful language that is child focused.

- Talk first with all of your children together. Explain what will change and what will stay the name.

- Don't make promises you cannot guarantee.

- Talk with extended family and friends to explain what is happening, and ask for their support. Establish boundaries if necessary.

CHAPTER 7

Sharing Information While Nesting

By now you know that without some mutual trust and good-enough communication, your nesting will be difficult, frustrating, and potentially unsuccessful. Sharing information about your children and your new living situation in respectful ways is central to the success of the nesting. In this chapter, you will learn about how your emotions affect your communication, how to communicate effectively, and what information needs to be shared while you are co-parenting and nesting in the family home. You will also find some tools to help with some structured checklists.

Practice Active Listening

Before we discuss talking and sharing information, let's focus on another skill that's just as vital: listening. The way in which you listen to someone else talk can have a significant impact on the tone and tenor of the conversation. Not making eye contact, sighing, rolling your eyes, and mentally planning your rebuttal while the other person is talking are listening habits many people have—but they're counterproductive to good communication.

As you and your partner navigate this new phase of life, a tool called active listening is one you can turn to again and again. In active listening, you are digesting what the other person is saying and asking questions when necessary. When your spouse is done talking, reflect back what you think you have understood and ask your spouse if you got it right—as in, "I'm hearing you say you think Ava is going to bed too late because her teacher says she's yawning in class. Is that right?" If not, let him or her explain it again. When you do understand it, you can truly say that you heard and understood the point he or she is making, and your partner will certainly appreciate that. When your partner feels that you have understood him or her, your partner will then be much more open to hearing what you have to say.

Remember, understanding is not necessarily agreeing. This is very important. You may think Ava is just bored in school, and you should certainly share your thoughts on the matter. If you and your spouse disagree on a topic, continue talking about it using active listening, and you are much more likely to reach common ground.

Why It's So Important to Communicate with Your Spouse

As you and your spouse rotate in and out of the house, you may be tempted to rely on your children for information, news, or updates. This is a burden your children should not have to carry, however. You need to be able to rely on direct communication from your spouse so that the transitions from off duty to on duty (or the reverse) will go smoothly. Aside from reducing your own stress, your efforts to communicate with your spouse directly, and not through your children, will let your children know that they can count on their parents to continue to co-parent them, even as they are separated or divorced.

Sometimes it seems like a chore to communicate directly with your spouse. Sometimes you may be too upset to talk to your co-parent, and other times you may feel that what you have to say isn't that important. Maybe you are worried that talking will lead to an argument. Maybe you feel your spouse is holding back information from you, and so you decide to withhold too. Unfortunately, *not* communicating is one way that parents sometimes act out their anger or other feelings.

Here are some of the problems with that tactic:

- Even not communicating is sending a message. Not communicating, and not sharing information, is, in fact, a communication. A negative one and possibly inflammatory, to be sure, but it's a type of communication.

- Your children will pick up on the tension between their parents when information is not shared or communication is disrespectful. Nonverbal communication is both normal and unavoidable. When you are upset or frustrated, this stress is communicated to your children nonverbally even if you don't say it aloud. They will feel it in the way you hug them, or simply by observing your facial expressions. Children know their parents' faces well, and it isn't possible to fully hide your feelings from them.

No matter how upset, angry, sad, or anxious you are, changing the pattern of communication between you will make everything else easier. It will help your children because stress is contagious. When you feel less distress, your children will absorb that from your calm tone of voice or your facial expression at the sound of your spouse's name. Even though it can be difficult, there are many techniques that can ease the flow of communication between you and your partner. Let's talk about some of them.

CASE IN POINT

Justin and Jess were nesting well, taking particular care to communicate regarding their daughter, Meghan, who suffered from anorexia. They had detailed agreements in their nesting agreement about regular communication after weight checks or meals that didn't go well.

When Meghan's brother, Sam, was caught with marijuana at school, however, Justin, who was on duty, agreed not to tell Jess. He agreed with Sam that Jess would probably overreact, so they colluded with each other to keep the secret. Justin went with Sam to meet the school principal, the school counselor, and the police officer who was assigned to the school. Justin organized all the logistics required by the diversion program at the local police station.

Jess knew nothing about this and had no idea what had happened until months later. She found out by accident when she ran into one of Sam's teachers who asked how the diversion program was going. This teacher didn't know about the secret, and Jess was floored.

Jess didn't want to end the nesting, but she was extremely upset at Sam and Justin. She called a meeting with a therapist, where she confronted both of them about what had happened.

This crisis in communication could have derailed the nesting, and Justin didn't want that to happen. Instead of becoming defensive, he told Jess, "I've felt bad about this ever since it happened, but I didn't know how to tell you. The longer I waited, the harder it was. I realize I made a bunch of very bad decisions and am very sorry about it. I'd like to make a new agreement: no secrets."

With some time and a few more sessions with their counselor, Jess and Justin were able to repair their communication. Furthermore, it was made very clear to Sam that there would be no more secrets or pitting one parent against the other. This actually reassured Sam that both of his parents were actively parenting him.

Remember to Practice "Good-Enough Communication"

Good-enough communication is as critical as trust to the success of nesting. Yet communication is a top problem among couples who are struggling to connect.

MOVING PAST OLD PROBLEMS

The most common complaint that couples bring to my therapy office is poor communication. I hear statements like the following:

- "He is just so defensive; I can't say anything! He takes everything so personally."

- "She nags me nonstop, and always wants to talk, talk, talk!"

- "He won't share anything with me and says he'll do things but never follows up."

- "She never compromises."

- "I never know what is going on with her. She just shuts down and withdraws for days at a time. She tells her friends more than she tells me."

- "She keeps bringing up old stuff from the past—why can't she just let it go? It isn't worth it to bring up issues, so we just shove it all under the rug."

If you and your partner struggled with communication problems during your marriage, they may get worse during your divorce when you feel you have nothing left to lose. The negative and harmful dynamics of your marital relationship can poison your separation, divorce, and postdivorce relationship.

The conflicts—whether they are openly expressed or not— are not healthy for you or your children, nor is it productive to continue to argue. It's important to focus on changing these dynamics, even if you decide not to nest.

IT REALLY IS POSSIBLE TO IMPROVE YOUR COMMUNICATION SKILLS, EVEN NOW

Despite how dire things might seem, you can improve how you communicate with your partner. In fact, during your separation, you'll finally have some respite from day-to-day conflict, and perhaps some relief from stress or indecision, and that might open up space for you to focus on better communication. Use this opportunity to look at how *you* can change the way you communicate with your partner. If you put effort into making some small changes, I promise that it will affect your partner too, even if your partner doesn't want to focus on these changes.

ADJUSTING YOUR COMMUNICATION GOALS

When you married, you wanted to know each other deeply, understand each other's emotions, ease each other's pain, and support each other's efforts. You were drawn to offer physical affection (this is also communication, of course) and demonstrate your commitment to the spouse's welfare. Ideally, you would ask questions, listen to your partner's needs, express your own needs, and work together to solve problems and set goals. Your goal was to try to make each other feel loved, respected, and understood. You would avoid lecturing, belittling, and judging.

When you have separated, this kind of intimate communication and connection is no longer your goal, unless both of you decide to work together to revive your relationship. The goal of good-enough communication during nesting is not so much about feelings but more about the pragmatic—about scheduling logistics, what's best for your children, and finances. Your goal is to "get the job done," as you nest, and work your way through your separation and potential divorce as co-parents.

Part of setting new goals is deciding *how much* to share. For example, if your child asks you questions about the separation or divorce, do you tell your co-parent? Do you share your responses to the child with your co-parent? Is it ever okay to keep your child's secrets from the other parent? This has to do with how cooperative you and your spouse are and how much communication you feel you want, need, or can handle.

KEY GOOD-ENOUGH COMMUNICATION TIPS

Following are some basic guidelines that you can follow to improve your communication while you nest. In many ways, this is how you would speak respectfully or communicate effectively with your business partner. One couple I counseled liked to say that their new role with their co-parent is to be "business partners in the business of raising our children." Putting yourself in this mindset might help you implement these ideas.

1. Listen to your spouse and repeat back what you understand. "I'm hearing that you…"

2. If you're upset, try to take time to breathe, calm down, and plan what you want to say before you start talking.

3. If you are having trouble staying calm in person, use email. But keep it short, cordial, and stick to information only. Write the message, then wait a few hours. Reread it, adjust as needed, and then hit Send.

4. Stick to sharing facts; don't vent about emotional issues to your partner. (Share those with a trusted friend or therapist.) Give information or ask a question ("Can you pick up the kids today?") in a neutral voice, a cordial, civil tone. Keep it short and to the point.

5. Don't respond every time you are triggered by something your partner says or does or doesn't do. Breathe and wait. Sleep on it. If an issue is escalating in the moment, suggest a break and separate.

6. Don't use "You never," or "You always" language. That's one of the quickest ways to a toxic conversation.

7. Don't post anything about your spouse, kids, divorce, or your social life unless your spouse has specifically agreed to it. Social media is a form of communication, and you need to be sure you and your spouse have a mutual understanding about what's acceptable and what's not. For example, posting a picture of your child's piano recital may seem innocuous to you, but it could upset your spouse if he or she wasn't in attendance. At the very least, plan to minimize your use of social media during this time of transition—and don't post anything about your spouse or the divorce.

Sharing Information about Your Children

As you and your spouse rotate in and out of the house, the transition can be seamless for your children if each of you catches the other up on how the children have been during that parent's on-duty time. This communication keeps everyone on the same page and reassures your children that both parents are working together and actively involved in parenting them.

One simple and useful tool is "Our Children's Day," a checklist to be completed by the parent going off duty and shared just before or at the point when the other parent is coming on duty. This checklist includes information such as updating your co-parent about your children's health, eating, sleeping, hygiene, mood, schoolwork, behavior, sibling relationships, and scheduling changes. While you're nesting, it would also include any information about the condition of the home, such as "The faucet is leaking, but the plumber is coming tomorrow between 1:00–3:00. Can you call him if you won't be here?" You can tailor this form as needed to fit your family and home situation.

OUR CHILDREN'S DAY

To be shared before the change of on-duty parent responsibility to have the information needed for a smooth transition.

- Health: Illnesses, prescriptions, etc.

  ....

- Eating: Leftovers, any new or unusual foods in the house

  ....

- Sleeping: Recent/daily, nighttime sleeping patterns, new issues, changes in bedtime rituals

  ....

- Hygiene: Recent activities, anything parents are tracking, e.g. toilet training for younger children, showering, self-care for older children, etc.

  ....

- Language (for younger children): New words, phrases, or expressions

  ....

- Emotional/Behavior/Mood: Tracking behaviors that parents are concerned about, e.g. clinginess, sadness, tantrums, or adjustment issues

  ....

- School/Academic: School-related/homework

  ....

- Social/Sibling Relationships

  ....

- New Experiences: Descriptions of events that your children might have had during your on-duty time that are important to remember together

  ....

- Scheduling Changes: Changes in the schedule that need to be planned for

  ....

- Issues Relating to the Home: Repairs, damages, maintenance, or any other problems that relate to the home, e.g. a leaky toilet, a broken appliance, etc.

  ....

The "Our Children's Day" tool makes it easier to share information without necessarily having direct contact, and it is therefore especially important in the early weeks and months when your emotions may be overwhelming and you're feeling fragile. You could email this to your co-parent before he or she comes on duty, or perhaps leave it on the kitchen counter. If you and your co-parent are able to speak on the phone, important information could be conveyed via a phone call or voice mail—but keep in mind that it is helpful to have a written record of the information to avoid misunderstandings.

Using Technology to Stay In Touch

There are a number of other tools and ways to share information in this digital age. Many nesting parents establish some guidelines as to when and how to use shared online calendars, texting, email, or voice mail, as well as expectations regarding response time. Here are some suggestions to consider.

SHARED ONLINE CALENDARS
Many parents have found that free shared online family calendars are very useful. This shared calendar will be the place where

you will note doctor's appointments, parent-teacher conferences, school project due dates, playdates, sports games, birthday parties, travel plans, and the like. Both parents will need to commit and be responsible for posting information in a timely fashion, and both parents need to monitor the calendar daily.

TEXTING—DO'S AND DON'TS

Texting is useful only for logistical issues, such as "I'm running ten minutes late," or "Got called into a meeting, can you get the kids?" Because it is instant and pops up on your spouse's phone, it's also useful in case of an emergency, such as "Jake fell at school, broke a tooth, and I'm on my way to the dentist." Texting generally requires an immediate response, or as soon as reasonably possible.

Texts should never be used for substantive issues, or "conversations." It is much too easy to miscommunicate or misunderstand a text message. Just stick to facts and keep it short. You can, however, text photos of the kids to your ex.

EMAILS AND RESPONSE TIME

Many parents use email for more substantive issues or questions. However, some parents are triggered or overwhelmed if they receive a lot of emails from their spouse. These parents might ask that the spouse consolidate the issues or questions and not send more than one email a day. Others prefer separate emails be sent for each question or issue, with the subject clear in the subject box. This way, the recipient can respond to one issue at a time. You and your spouse will need to decide what will work best for you.

Your nesting agreement should include your expectations regarding response time for emails. Generally, I suggest that at a minimum you acknowledge receipt of the email within twenty-four hours. If you can't respond to the issue or question, let your spouse know when you believe you will be able to respond.

KEEPING IT RESPECTFUL: BIFF

I counsel parents to review what they have written, whether a text or an email, to check that it is Brief, Informative, Firm, and Friendly (BIFF) before sending. This mnemonic was developed by Bill Eddy, a social worker and attorney who specializes in difficult or high-conflict divorces.

If you have any doubt about whether your message is appropriate, don't send it. Wait a few hours or overnight, and review what you have written again. Some people ask a friend to review their emails, particularly if they are addressing something sensitive or are feeling particularly upset. It's better to avoid sending an angry message in the first place than dealing with the aftermath of a hostile email.

CASE IN POINT

Olivia and Barb were nesting with their adopted twin boys. In their nesting agreement, Olivia agreed not to introduce the boys to her new relationship for at least a year. She had also agreed to ensure their children were ready and rested for school during her on-duty weekends. One day, however, the boys came home and told Barb, who had come on duty, that Olivia had allowed them to stay up late to watch a movie on Sunday night. Barb was furious and reacted immediately by writing this email:

I can't believe you let the kids watch TV till 10 when you KNEW they had school the next day. Don't you realize how IRRESPONSIBLE that is?? Did you think that the show was an appropriate one for them? Your judgment has always stunk, you know? They came home exhausted and cranky today, and wouldn't stop fighting with each other. Do you ever stop to think about how I have to CLEAN UP your messes? You promised to make sure they were rested and ready for school but I guess I just can't trust you. You're probably going to introduce your new GIRLFRIEND to them too, right? This nesting thing is NOT going to work with you being so IMMATURE and IRRESPONSIBLE. So. What do you have to say for yourself, now?

Fortunately, she never sent this email, but she did feel a little better having written it. She was aware that she was in "reaction mode" in a fit of rage, rather than "responding mode." So, she sent it to her best friend and her friend was able to calm her down. A few hours later, Barb wrote and sent a new email:

Olivia, the kids came home really tired today. They said you'd let them watch a movie last night and so they got to stay up past their bedtime. I would appreciate it if you would keep our agreement and get them to bed earlier on school nights. I don't mind if you let them stay up a little later if they don't have school the next morning. Hope that works for you.

This calm but firm tone worked, and Olivia wrote back simply:

My bad. Sorry. Won't do that again.

Check In to Assess Nesting

It's a good idea to check in periodically with your spouse to discuss your observations and impressions of nesting in general. See if you agree about how the nesting agreement is working.

- How is the co-parenting working out and how are the children doing with the changes?
- Do you need to revisit any parts of your agreement?
- How is the nesting affecting your relationship with each other? You may see some improvements, or perhaps none.

If you need to make adjustments based on your observations, go ahead and do so.

Off-Duty Communication with Your Children

You and your spouse should discuss and agree on when and how your children may communicate with their off-duty parent. If you are co-parenting well, you may be flexible about phone calls or texts to and from the off-duty parent and the child. Some families have a ritual of a good-night phone call with the off-duty parent. For some children, however, this may actually be upsetting. Some children just don't want to talk on the phone at all. And some on-duty parents who want more separation may find these calls intrusive, or resent the children having phone contact with the off-duty parent.

I suggest that you grant the children the option that is least stressful to them—even if it's difficult for you. This means that you might have to accept less contact even if you miss your children terribly and long to hear their voices. On the other hand, if your children miss you when you are off duty, accept their need for contact and allow (or even encourage) it.

A word of caution: There will be times when your children are mad at you, and they might reach out to the off-duty parent to enlist help or support. Your children might call you when you are off duty to complain, request that you overrule a decision, or ask to be "rescued" from the on-duty parent. Kids with their own cell phones may call their off-duty parent impulsively, and this often stirs up trouble. Generally, it is best to let the on-duty parent handle the issue unless there is a safety issue. If you get involved without the consent of your co-parent, you will be seen as disruptive, intrusive, manipulative, and currying favor with your children.

CASE IN POINT

Justin and Jess's son Sam called Jess because Justin had grounded him for the weekend. He called Jess almost in tears.

"Dad is forcing me to miss my school dance!"

Justin could have reached out to Jess for support or counsel regarding the discipline he wanted to impose, but he didn't.

"You'll need to talk to Dad about this," she said instead. "If he wants to talk with me about it, he'll call. Otherwise, he's in charge."

Jess avoided getting into the middle of the problem between Sam and his father. This wasn't easy for Jess because she didn't feel close to Sam after the drug incident. She might have tried to rescue Sam in order to reconnect with him. But it was important for Sam to know that his parents would not allow him to pit one parent against the other.

Sharing Information with Others

There are no doubt other caregivers in your children's lives who will need to know some details of your arrangement, and they will need to keep you apprised of issues as well.

SCHOOL

Your children's school may need to know your family's nesting schedule so that they know who is on duty, especially if your kids are young. They should know whom to contact for pickup or in case your children get hurt or are ill. You should also request that all information for parents is emailed to both parents.

Your children will benefit when their teachers know which parent is picking them up, and which parent is available to help with homework. Teachers are part of your children's support network, particularly before they are in high school.

OTHER CAREGIVERS

There may be others who need updates about the children while you are nesting, including daycare providers, therapists, other family members, and anyone else in their extended support network. Out of respect for your spouse and your children, what you share should probably be strictly on a "need to know" basis. For example, if you have a child who has begun to wet the bed again, the therapist should know this. The therapist who is treating your child is likely trained to help with a child's regression during divorce. But perhaps your teenage after-school babysitter, soccer coach, or other carpool drivers do not need to know.

KEY POINTS TO REMEMBER

- You can't *not* communicate!

- Practice fact-based, neutral communication with your partner. Keep things Brief, Informative, Firm, and Friendly.

- If you are feeling emotional, give yourself time and space to calm down before communicating.

- Get in the habit of sharing information with your co-parent about your children and the home whenever you go off duty. This is reassuring for your children.

- Decide how you will use texting, emails, a calendar, and other communication tools.

- Make an agreement regarding off-duty communication with your children.

Part Three

Moving Into the Future

IN THIS PART, we will focus on improving your emotional (and physical) health in this new phase of your life. The logistics of nesting, which we've covered in Parts 1 and 2, are very important, but so is the process of dealing with the many intense feelings you're experiencing. Most people have received very little instruction on talking about feelings and moving past them. Just as you learned about healthy eating and exercise, you need to learn how to take care of your emotional health.

After we address self-care, we'll look at when and how your nesting will end. We will think about how you will make the decisions for your next steps, whether you choose to reconcile or to divorce. You'll learn the many specific considerations for each option. Finally, you'll find some tips for helping your children move into the next phase of your family's life.

CHAPTER 8

Coping with Your Feelings

There is no right or wrong way to feel as you deal with the changes you're experiencing. In the early stages of separation, you might feel a sense of surreal shock. Even if you made the decision to separate, it may be hard to believe it is actually happening. One of my clients told me she felt "stupefied" and that she was in a "fog." A part of you may feel a sense of relief that the arguing has ended, or that you (or your partner) have finally made the decision. Another part of you may feel overwhelmed with grief that the hopes and dreams you had once cherished haven't worked out as you imagined. You may cry easily and frequently. Yet another part of you may feel paralyzing anxiety about what the future holds.

No matter what your current emotional state is, it's important to learn how to talk about it so you can begin to heal and move into the next phase of your life. Identifying and naming your feelings will help you work through them so that you can move on in a healthy way. By being able to self-assess your emotional state, you will be more aware of how your emotions are affecting your nesting relationship.

It's Normal to Feel Overwhelmed by Life's Changes

While you're nesting, you are probably processing how your marriage came to this juncture. While caring for your children, you'll also need to cope with all of your emotions, from rage to grief, from fear to hope, or from guilt to relief. You may feel exhausted or you may feel reenergized. There's no way to predict what you will be feeling and how you will work through the emotions.

There's also no timetable for getting through the emotions. Your emotions will be complicated, and it will take a while to feel calm enough to make good decisions about the future of your marriage. Nesting will give you that time so that you can decide what comes next with composure and clear thinking.

Maybe you are thinking about what went wrong and what would need to change in order to reconcile. You may be reflecting on your own behavior and decisions during the marriage and wondering if you can repair your mistakes. You may be identifying what it is that you want and need in your relationship and from your partner. You may have begun counseling with your spouse with the goal of determining the future of your marriage. You may have sought help from a therapist to clarify your own feelings and thoughts.

Your day-to-day emotional life might feel different as well (in addition to the logistical changes you have made related to separation and nesting). You may have a hard time keeping track of your days and schedule. Time may feel like it has slowed down or sped up. You may feel lost or question your spiritual faith. You wonder when you will get your energy back—you will!

With all of these emotions, it shouldn't be a surprise that you may find it difficult or impossible to concentrate or to get anything done. You feel forgetful and wonder if you are losing your mind. You may obsess about what is happening and feel unable to focus on anything else. You may pull away from friends and family, isolating yourself, then feeling deep loneliness. On the other hand, you might throw yourself into something that distracts you from your feelings, such as work or a new relationship. This may be exciting and lighten your mood. Your life has been changed in ways you're only starting to realize, and it's all right to feel confused about where you stand.

Struggling with a sense of betrayal, another part of you may be enraged with your spouse and with the world. There might even be physical changes as well: You may be unable to relax, feeling restless and agitated. You may experience a loss or increase in appetite, depleted energy levels, troubled sleep, headaches or stomach aches, or be more prone to catching a cold or infection.

CASE IN POINT

Clancy grew up in a poor family but had built his own successful business and was proud of his successes. He later married a wealthy woman with a trust fund, and they raised children. Clancy looked forward to spending more time with his wife now that the kids were in high school. When their marriage ended, Clancy couldn't understand why his wife wanted this divorce. He was haunted by images of living in a basement room with no windows. He couldn't sleep or eat, and he began to miss work due to his exhaustion. His soon-to-be ex-wife recognized that he was deeply depressed and wanted to reassure him. She often told him that she would never allow him to become destitute. This was not only because she genuinely cared about his welfare, but also because of their children who would be upset to see their father living in poverty.

The outcome was very different from Clancy's imagined destitution. His wife's compassion and verbal reassurances were helpful, and her generosity in the final settlement, through a collaborative divorce process, did begin to restore his hope for the future. When I checked in with them a year after their divorce, they had just returned from a family vacation with their two teenaged children. Clancy was living in a comfortable home near his ex-spouse and had been able to rebuild his business as he recovered from his depression.

Both Parties Are in Pain

Some people in this state of upheaval begin to wonder if their spouse is better off than they are. The answer is probably no. Understandably, emotions run high during a separation and divorce, whether or not it was your decision to separate. Many life event stress scales rate divorce as the second most stressful life event; only the death of a spouse (or a child) is more stressful. You and your spouse are both experiencing a life crisis, though you may be experiencing it in different ways. Neither of you is at your best, and in fact, you or your spouse may be behaving in ways that you have never seen or predicted or experienced. You may feel volatile, depressed, exhausted, or paralyzed by fear. It may feel overwhelming just to get through your usual daily activities or even to get out of bed. It's important to remember that this is a difficult time for both of you—no matter which of you initiated the separation. And it is important to remember that things will get better over time.

IF YOU ENDED THE MARRIAGE

I've heard people say that the person who ends the marriage is always the happy one. This is an inaccurate oversimplification. Even if you are the one who made the decision to end the marriage, your emotions will be intense for quite a while. You may be feeling relief, but may also feel grief, anger, fear, shame, or guilt. Some people consider their decision for months or years and are relieved to have started the process, but finally making that decision is gut-wrenching. It can feel like a death, and in fact, it is the death of your hopes and dreams from the earlier days of your relationship.

I've also heard people say that if one person has started an affair, then ended the marriage, he or she is probably happy. This too is not always true. The affair may have been the passport out of an unhappy marriage, and for a while, it might be a welcome distraction from the pain of the separation. But even if the new relationship seems thrilling and has the potential to last, there are almost always feelings of remorse, guilt, sadness, and many other emotions.

IF YOUR PARTNER INITIATED THE SEPARATION

If you aren't the one to make the decision to separate, you may be feeling shocked if you did not see it coming. You trusted that the problems would eventually work themselves out or thought you would address them "later" when the kids were grown. You may have been in denial about the issues, or your spouse may not have shared his or her feelings about the marriage, so you didn't know that he or she was unhappy. You may feel betrayed, furious, grief-stricken, and many other feelings. You may feel guilty that you didn't try hard enough. You may fear for your future. It's difficult to even *identify* your specific feelings when you are overwhelmed with so many emotions!

Boosting Your Emotional Vocabulary

Learning to understand and move through all these emotions you're feeling will help you cope with the separation and will boost your chances of successful nesting. To deal with your emotions, it often helps to accurately name them. This is a basic skill that's important because when you can name them, they feel less out of control and more manageable. As you begin to be able to cope with and manage your feelings, you'll find that expressing thoughts, feelings, needs, and wants is an important part of separation and nesting, such as the following:

- Good-enough communication
- Building trust with your spouse while nesting
- Being able to talk about your feelings with trusted adults or a therapist

When I work with children, I often need to help them develop an emotional vocabulary because it's not a skill taught anywhere else. The general categories may seem childlike, but don't give this section short shift. Improving your emotional vocabulary will help you now and throughout your life, no matter your age. And once you can name your emotions, you can find ways to manage them.

Developing your emotional vocabulary and expressing your emotions often means that your negative or harmful marital dynamics will also change. As your communication skills improve, your post-separation relationship, and your children, will benefit. There will be less stress, fewer conflicts, and your nesting will be much more rewarding. With good use of your new emotional vocabulary, you may find that all your relationships improve! At that point, you'll be able to more easily go through the legal divorce process with the myriad chores and decisions that are required.

The English language is rich with feeling-words, with subtle nuances, shades of meaning and intensity. It may feel like you have a stew of emotions, all mixed together, and that is perfectly normal. Humans are able to experience many emotions at the same time, even seemingly contradictory emotions. For example, you may feel relief and anxiety at the same time, or heartbroken and also hopeful. Look at the following lists of words and see which ones resonate for you.

YOUR EMOTIONAL VOCABULARY LIST

ANGER, APATHY, AND HATRED		
Soft Anger, Apathy, and Hatred		
Annoyed	Cranky	Impatient
Apathetic	Critical	Indifferent
Bored	Cross	Irritated
Certain	Detached	Peeved
Cold	Displeased	Rankled
Crabby	Frustrated	
Medium Anger, Apathy, and Hatred		
Affronted	Bristling	Mad
Aggravated	Exasperated	Offended
Angry	Incensed	Resentful
Antagonized	Indignant	Riled Up
Arrogant	Inflamed	Sarcastic
Intense Anger, Apathy, and Hatred		
Aggressive	Hateful	Seething
Appalled	Hostile	Spiteful
Belligerent	Irate	Vengeful
Bitter	Livid	Vicious
Contemptuous	Menacing	Vindictive
Disgusted	Outraged	Violent
Enraged	Ranting	
Furious	Raving	

SHAME AND GUILT

Soft Shame and Guilt

Abashed	Flustered	Self-Conscious
Awkward	Hesitant	Speechless
Discomfited	Humble	Withdrawn
Flushed	Reticent	

Medium Shame and Guilt

Ashamed	Guilty	Remorseful
Chagrined	Humbled	Reproachful
Contrite	Intimidated	Rueful
Culpable	Penitent	Sheepish
Embarrassed	Regretful	

Intense Shame and Guilt

Belittled	Guilt-Stricken	Self-Flagellating
Degraded	Humiliated	Shamefaced
Demeaned	Mortified	Stigmatized
Disgraced	Ostracized	
Guilt-Ridden	Self-Condemning	

FEAR, ANXIETY, AND PANIC

Soft Fear, Anxiety, and Panic

Alert	Disquieted	Intuitive
Apprehensive	Doubtful	Leery
Cautious	Edgy	Pensive
Concerned	Fidgety	Shy
Confused	Hesitant	Timid
Curious	Indecisive	Uneasy
Disconcerted	Insecure	Watchful
Disoriented	Instinctive	

Medium Fear, Anxiety, and Panic

Afraid	Jumpy	Suspicious
Alarmed	Nervous	Unnerved
Anxious	Perturbed	Unsettled
Aversive	Rattled	Wary
Distrustful	Shaky	Worried
Fearful	Startled	

Intense Fear, Anxiety, and Panic

Filled with Dread	Paralyzed	Shocked
Horrified	Petrified	Terrorized
Panicked	Phobic	

JEALOUSY AND ENVY

Soft Jealousy and Envy

Disbelieving	Insecure	Suspicious
Distrustful	Protective	Vulnerable

Medium Jealousy and Envy

Covetous	Desirous	Jealous
Demanding	Envious	Threatened

Intense Jealousy and Envy

Avaricious	Greedy	Possessive
Gluttonous	Green with Envy	Resentful
Grasping	Persistently Jealous	

HAPPINESS, CONTENTMENT, AND JOY

Soft Happiness, Contentment, and Joy

Amused	Hopeful	Peaceful
Calm	Inspired	Smiling
Encouraged	Jovial	Upbeat
Friendly	Open	

Medium Happiness, Contentment, and Joy

Cheerful	Gratified	Playful
Contented	Happy	Pleased
Delighted	Healthy Self-Esteem	Proud
Excited	Joyful	Rejuvenated
Fulfilled	Lively	Satisfied
Glad	Merry	
Gleeful	Optimistic	

Intense Happiness, Contentment, and Joy

Awe-Filled	Euphoric	Overjoyed
Blissful	Exhilarated	Radiant
Ecstatic	Giddy	Rapturous
Egocentric	Jubilant	Self-Aggrandized
Elated	Manic	Thrilled
Enthralled	Overconfident	

SADNESS, GRIEF, AND DEPRESSION

Soft Sadness, Grief, and Depression

Contemplative	Grounded	Regretful
Disappointed	Listless	Wistful
Disconnected	Low	
Distracted	Steady	

Medium Sadness, Grief, and Depression

Dejected	Forlorn	Sad
Discouraged	Gloomy	Sorrowful
Dispirited	Grieving	Weepy
Down	Heavy-Hearted	World-Weary
Downtrodden	Melancholy	
Drained	Mournful	

Intense Sadness, Grief, and Depression

Anguished	Despairing	Hopeless
Bereaved	Despondent	Inconsolable
Bleak	Grief-Stricken	Morose
Depressed	Heartbroken	

DEPRESSION AND SUICIDAL URGES

Soft Depression and Suicidal Urges

Apathetic	Dispirited	Lethargic
Constantly Irritated, Angry, or Enraged (see the previous Anger list)	Feeling Worthless	Listless
	Flat	Melancholy
	Helpless	Pessimistic
	Humorless	Purposeless
Depressed	Impulsive	Withdrawn
Discouraged	Indifferent	
Disinterested	Isolated	

Medium Depression and Suicidal Urges

Bereft	Empty	Overwhelmed
Crushed	Fatalistic	Passionless
Desolate	Hopeless	Pleasureless
Despairing	Joyless	Sullen
Desperate	Miserable	
Drained	Morbid	

Intense Depression and Suicidal Urges

NOTE: Be sure to seek immediate medical help if you find yourself in this category. **The National Suicide Hotline is (800) 273-8255.**

Agonized	Doomed	Self-Destructive
Anguished	Gutted	Suicidal
Bleak	Nihilistic	Tormented
Death-Seeking	Numbed	Tortured
Devastated	Reckless	

CASE IN POINT

Brad had intended to nest until their son was at least nineteen. However, he felt manipulated and exploited when Emma kept asking to change their schedule. When Brad was upset at Emma, he briefly looked at this list and took a few long breaths and a short walk. He then counted to ten, planned what he would say, and was able to convey his emotions (disappointment, annoyance) in a way that Emma could take it in. Then he was able to request that she respect his need for a consistent schedule in order to keep his job. She acknowledged that many of her requests were not critical, that they were "wants" and not "needs" and that she could be more flexible. Together they brainstormed some other options when Emma wanted to make a change in the schedule.

Let Go of Your Anger

Anger is one of the main categories of emotions you're likely experiencing. It's also one that you should really focus on addressing because holding on to anger only prolongs your pain. Anger is the armor we wear when we don't want to feel our sadness. And, unfortunately, your anger is likely to provoke arguments or conflicts with your spouse, whereas your sadness will probably be less disruptive. If you're able to let go of your anger, not only will you feel better, but also your communication will be more respectful, and nesting will be more likely to succeed. There may have been many challenges, betrayals, or losses in your marriage. If you are able to put them all behind you, or find other adults to talk with, you'll be able to focus on the present, your children, and your recovery.

FORGIVING YOUR SPOUSE...AND YOURSELF

One path toward getting past anger is to forgive your spouse. This may seem impossible when you first separate, but over time forgiving your spouse will let you move on with a more peaceful heart. Know that forgiving your spouse doesn't mean that what she or he did was acceptable—it simply means that you are not going to dwell on that pain any longer. Holding on to anger punishes you and the other person, and it eventually becomes toxic. There is a wise saying: "Anger corrodes the container it's in."

Forgiving is not a one-time action. Rather it is a practice, a process, where you gradually learn to let go of your anger by managing your emotions when you are triggered. You learn to focus on yourself, your future, and your strengths. It's okay if you don't feel ready to forgive just yet—you may need more time to think about and process the unhealthy dynamics in your marriage, likely with a therapist. But you can begin to plant the seeds of forgiveness, by reminding yourself that you will eventually be able to let go of your hurt, pain, and anger. As you work to forgive your spouse, you might need to accept your own role in the problems of the relationship and forgive yourself as well.

If you are angry at yourself for "failing," try to change that mindset. While the relationship may have failed, you are not a failure. Perhaps you were raised to believe that you are solely responsible for the health of the marriage, and you may think that this separation is your "fault." Remember that a relationship takes two people, and you both have some responsibility in the separation. Try to avoid putting yourself down and reinforcing a negative self-image. Not being able to fix your marriage does *not* mean that you are a failure. Read that sentence again! *You* are not a failure if you believe that the marriage is over. Sometimes, even if both spouses want the marriage to survive, it may not be possible to fix your marriage. In fact, even when both work hard to fix the marriage, it may not be possible. I once worked with a couple who spent many years in couples counseling, learning communication skills and addressing problems with their disparate parenting styles. While these did improve their relationship, there were too many other areas of conflict and resentment. Ultimately they were exhausted, hopeless, no longer in love, and they gave up.

Moving past anger is not easy, but it's a necessary part of your emotional healing. Forgiving the lies and misdemeanors, the betrayals and the hurts, *and* accepting your part of the blame and forgiving yourself opens up your mind and heart to a new chapter in your life. The next chapter offers a wealth of ideas for healthy ways to focus on improving your mind, body, and spirit during this time of transition.

KEY POINTS TO REMEMBER

- Your emotions are probably in upheaval now. You might feel a confusing range of emotions that change from day to day.

- Both you and your partner are dealing with the effects of this separation. Trying to figure out who's happy and who's not is not a worthwhile exercise.

- Identifying and naming your emotions accurately will help you manage them better. You'll also be able to talk about them in a more comprehensive manner, whether with other trusted adults or a therapist.

- Most separating couples are dealing with anger in some form, and it is the most disruptive to your nesting. Learning to let go of anger (or to release it elsewhere) will allow you to move past this phase of your life.

CHAPTER 9

Taking Care of Yourself

During a separation or divorce, the pressures can become overwhelming. You are learning to be a solo parent and a co-parent at a time when you may be flooded emotionally. You're working hard to keep your children's lives as stable as possible while feeling that your own life is quite unstable. You are trying to make sound decisions at a time when you are distracted and having trouble concentrating, and it's hard to think things through.

We exhaust ourselves caring for others, often while neglecting our own needs. This is where self-care, or intentional practices that recharge your mental and emotional batteries and nourish your body, are crucial. In this chapter, we will focus on the importance of self-care during the nesting period, and what typical experiences signal the need for help. We'll then look at the many ways you can take care of your own mental, emotional, physical, and spiritual health during this transition from being a couple to being a co-parent.

The Importance of Self-Care

Whether trying to get ahead, or simply survive from one day to the next, it's easy to overlook your own emotional and physical burnout. When you experience a loss, such as a separation or a divorce, that depletion is amplified. The need for self-care becomes even more pressing.

The concept of self-care is not new. It started as a medical term, as early as the late nineteenth century, and was picked up later in the women's, civil rights, and LGBTQ movements. In the last twenty-five years, the concept of self-care has become enmeshed with the growth of evidence-based positive psychology and preventative medicine.

Children do pretty well when it comes to self-care, since adults respond and support them. When they're hungry, they let you know, and you feed them. When they're tired, they let you know that too, and you ensure they have a place to rest. They also have a strong drive to learn: Their instinct to socialize is innate, and they play. While they may not know this, play is a form of self-care. Play is simply doing something for the fun of it. There's no goal other than the pure joy of the activity. But if you ask adults when the last time they played was, they'll probably be stumped. Do you remember the last time you played, laughed out loud, or did something silly, just for the sheer pleasure of it? For many, the answer is no.

The truth is that despite all of the research proving how beneficial self-care is to our lives, most of us ignore our own physical, mental, and psychological needs.

CASE IN POINT

When Jack and Allie separated, Allie worried about how her children would adjust. She wanted to make up for her sense of "loss of family" by being the "perfect mom." She baked cookies at least once a week and went to every one of her girls' games. She distracted herself from her grief by scrubbing the house from top to bottom every time she came on duty.

And when she was off duty, she spent time reading everything she could find about divorce and child development. She "forgot" to exercise and didn't make time to see friends or family. She gave up her hikes with her best friend so that she could surf the Internet, looking for help for her marriage. She was so focused on prioritizing her children that she neglected herself. She was worn out. She'd put so many things on her to-do list that there was no room for self-care.

That is, until she had a minor car accident and realized her mind had wandered so far away that she didn't pay attention to keeping herself safe on the road. This was a wake-up call for her. "What if the kids had been in the car?" she asked herself. She sat down with her therapist and made two lists: what she could take off her to-do list, "That stuff can wait," she said, and what self-care activities she could schedule into her days.

Self-Care and Health During Nesting

During a separation or divorce, your stress may seem crushing at times, and you can feel as though you're on an emotional rollercoaster. This is when you most need to incorporate self-care into your daily life. In fact, your health depends on it. Countless studies show that stress can cause many health problems, from cardiovascular disease to autoimmune illness.

While your health should be a compelling enough reason to focus on self-care, it is also crucial in ensuring that you are fully present for your children during nesting. Your ability to concentrate, think clearly, make decisions, cope with challenges, and manage your ups and downs are all affected by self-care (or lack of it). You may have heard it said that "Self-care is not selfish," or "You can't help anyone else on the plane until you put on your own oxygen mask." These are the slogans of self-care advocates.

CASE IN POINT

Brad had his hands full with work and caring for his disabled son. He'd been experiencing physical symptoms, such as agitation, insomnia, and night sweats, for some time, but he ignored them. "I don't have time to go to the doctor," he said. Instead, he ran five miles a day, trying to outrun his stress. His anxiety rose so much that every time he went on duty he experienced heart palpitations. He was losing weight, which he thought was a good thing until he realized that he was getting weaker. Then he noticed that his hair was falling out at an alarming rate. When his hands were shaking so badly that he spilled his coffee, he finally made the decision to call the doctor. He was diagnosed with Graves' disease, a thyroid disorder often caused by stress, but fortunately, he was able to be treated and recover. While in treatment, he had to give up his on-duty time, and Emma stepped in to cover for him.

Once Brad had regained his health, he reflected that he'd been unable to be fully present with William due to the nervous energy and restlessness caused by his hyperthyroid condition. In addition, he realized that he'd been less patient and more irritable than usual, with both Emma and William. If that had continued, Emma might have called off the nesting. He also learned that untreated Graves' disease can be fatal, and that if he had not gone to the doctor, he could have died. He knew that neglecting his symptoms had risked both the nesting and his health.

Emotional Days of the Early Stages of Separation

In Chapter 8, you learned more about the many emotional and physical reactions you can experience during the early stages of separation or divorce. From guilt and sadness to difficulty eating or concentrating, a lot can go on under the surface.

It's important to remember that these are normal reactions to an abnormal (for you) situation. Extreme changes, loss, and crisis trigger extreme emotional reactions. While this is predictable, what you experience will be unique to you, your personality and history, and how you usually cope with crisis in your life. Although the emotions are normal, these emotions are your body's and psyche's way of asking for help, and self-care will be one of the first and most important steps you take to begin your recovery.

If you have a therapist, or if you have never been in counseling, this is also an excellent time to seek some additional support. As intense as these reactions are, they will ease with the passage of time and the resolution of many of the issues raised by separation and divorce.

What Is Self-Care?

When you're in a crisis, you are understandably desperate to feel better. You want to believe all those advertisements you see that claim that certain products will boost self-confidence or reduce anxiety. Self-care is sometimes equated with "treating yourself" or "you deserve" whatever product is being promoted.

The truth is that self-care simply refers to all of the habits, routines, and personal and idiosyncratic ways we deal with crisis, stress, unhappiness, illness, and depression—the mental, physical, emotional, and spiritual problems in our lives. Some of us engage in negative coping strategies that are actually destructive—such as abusing drugs or alcohol. They simply anesthetize feelings, wipe you out, and leave you with a physical and psychological hangover that makes your life worse than ever. This is not self-care. Beneficial self-care choices, on the other hand, promote a healthy body and positive outlook.

The following sections outline dozens of ideas for healthy self-care. Every person is different, so pick and choose the ideas that appeal to you. Be patient with yourself throughout the healing process, and focus on developing and sticking to the self-care strategies that work best for you and your situation. Your off-duty time will be the perfect opportunity to try out these different activities. A final note: You will see that virtually none of these ideas cost money. Of course, you *can* spend money to treat yourself to a spa day or new outfit, but it's not necessary for self-care.

Mental Self-Care Ideas

Mental self-care includes any activities that reduce the ongoing chatter in your head and recharge your mind. This self-care will help you focus, plan, better manage time, remember things, and make decisions—all important parts of setting up a nesting arrangement, adjusting to being a solo parent, and working through any legal processes with your spouse. Here are some ways to practice mental self-care:

1. **Avoid people who make you feel bad about yourself.** Seek out people who support and encourage you, and take a step back from those who criticize you or discourage you in your goals. Clients have often told me that it was during their divorce that they found out who their true friends were.

2. **Say no.** Turn down new requests when you don't feel up to them. Don't be worried about letting someone down: Sometimes you simply can't do more than you're already doing. You may also want to cut back on unnecessary responsibilities if you can. For example, one client reduced her carpooling commitment when she was first adapting to her nesting arrangement.

3. **Challenge negative thoughts.** When you're anxious, it's human nature to imagine the very worst possible outcome, which only makes you feel worse. Any self-critical thought, or one that includes the word "should," is a red flag. Step back and look around for concrete evidence of what's really going on to change those dark imaginings into reality-based thoughts.

4. **Try something new.** Test your culinary skills with a new recipe, or check out a museum or park. Learning a new skill or trying a new activity stimulates your brain and energizes your mind. You may feel curious, proud, or simply interested, and an energized brain is a healthy brain.

5. **Schedule time for nothing.** Mark some blank space in your calendar where nothing at all is scheduled. Use that time to take a walk around the block, or take a nap. Essentially, just do only what you really enjoy. Don't feel guilty about that!

6. **Read a good book.** Pick up a bestseller, or sign up for free audible lending books at your local library. A good book is not only a distraction from your troubling thoughts, but it also gives you the pleasure of a good story. Pleasure, play, and laughter are all good for your mental health.

7. **Go to bed and get up at the same time every day.** Your life will feel more balanced and stable if you have a regular sleep schedule, and you will feel more alert, clearheaded, and energized in the morning.

8. **Journal.** Let your hand go on autopilot, writing down whatever comes to mind. The goal is not to record your activities, but rather to allow your thoughts and feelings to flow onto the page, without any judgment or censoring. Some studies show that writing with a pen or pencil accesses a different part of your brain than typing on a keyboard. Journaling with a pen and paper may be more liberating because it forces you to slow down and think about what you are writing. You are more able to access thoughts and feelings and focus on what is most important to you. According to a study in

Developmental Neuropsychology, writing by hand activates your brain's motor cortex in a similar way to meditation.

9. **Limit social media/screen time.** Social media can be especially toxic when you see your friends (or your spouse) looking like their lives are perfect. (They are not!) Social media might deceive you into thinking that everyone else's life is better than your own. In addition, it is easy to isolate yourself and get pulled into hours of computer games and surfing the Internet, rather than getting out and doing something physical or social with actual people.

10. **Explore a new area.** Get a guidebook to your area and check out someplace you have never been. No matter where you live, there are always things to discover.

Emotional Self-Care Ideas

Emotional self-care includes any activity that helps you ease negative feelings or stimulate positive feelings. Managing your emotions through these practices will support a positive nesting experience because you interact more calmly with your co-parent and model self-care for your children. Here are some examples of emotional self-care:

1. **Cry/scream it out.** If you need to cry or scream, find a private space to let it out. No one will hear you, and it feels cathartic to release those feelings. One client told me that she simply went into her car for a good cry with the windows rolled up.

2. **Take deep breaths.** The quickest way to help both your mind and body slow down is to do some deep belly breaths. Just three deep breaths can make a big change in how you feel. Your body simply can't be anxious and relaxed at the same time. It is biologically impossible!

3. **Listen to music.** Try something upbeat, like soul, musicals, rhythm and blues, pop, Cajun, opera—whatever rouses your spirits.

4. **Visualize a peaceful place or loving experience that you've had.** Hold the image for five minutes, focusing on the different colors, sounds, and sensations, allowing yourself to be completely absorbed by the good feelings that are evoked.

5. **Write a thank-you note.** Let people know how much you appreciate them. It will bring a little cheer to their day—and yours.

6. **Watch a good movie.** Whether it's a new release or one you've seen before and still love, movies can make you smile or laugh even when you're dealing with a difficult situation in life.

7. **Create positive affirmations.** A simple, self-affirming phrase has the power to reduce stress and overcome negative thoughts. Write some positive affirmations on sticky notes and put them on your bathroom mirror where you will see them each day. If you need ideas, you can find thousands of affirmations online.

8. **Color.** Many have said that adult coloring books help them feel grounded, mindful, calm, and creative. If you enjoy

painting, you can also take out those brushes, oils, or water-colors and get something down on canvas.

9. **Do something nice for someone else.** Drop off a batch of cookies to a neighbor or write a glowing review online for a favorite restaurant. It will make you feel good, and they will too.

10. **Spend time with a loved one or pet.** This can be a family member, close friend, or even a beloved pet. Whatever you do with them during this time, you will find that you feel better.

Physical Self-Care Ideas

Physical self-care includes any activity that nourishes your body. You need your stamina and endurance to make your way through a separation and to foster a healthy environment while you are nesting. Staying fit and healthy will make your nesting more satisfying. The moving in and out of the home as you rotate on and off duty takes a certain amount of physical strength too. And when you feel good physically, you also feel better mentally and emotionally. Here are examples of physical self-care:

1. **Stretch.** When you get up in the morning, take a minute to stretch your back, legs, feet, hands, and neck. Consult a physical therapist or look online for proper stretching techniques.

2. **Drink plenty of water.** Follow any exercise or stretching sessions with a full glass of water, then drink several other glasses over the course of your day.

3. **Mindful breathing.** Breathing brings oxygen into your body and brain and increases your energy. Sit for two minutes and just focus on your breathing. Every following day make the time you spend practicing deep breaths one minute longer. While three deep breaths will help you calm down in a tense moment, mindful breathing for a few minutes will help you feel more grounded and energized all day.

4. **Take a walk.** If you have a dog, take your pet with you! If you are not usually a walker, start with a ten-minute walk and increase the amount gradually every day.

5. **Go for a run or jog.** Get that "runner's high": the increase in feel-good endorphins that comes from exercise. Cycling and swimming work too.

6. **Get out in nature.** Feel the sunshine on your face and breathe in the fresh air. Go somewhere outside—a beach, meadow, mountain trail, or the woods—and take in the beauty around you.

7. **Practice yoga.** Yoga is great for strength, flexibility, and balance. If you've never done yoga, now is a good time to try a beginner's class. Do not judge yourself when you get there: Yoga is a practice, not a competition. You can also find many excellent online yoga videos to do in your own living space.

8. **Get a massage.** A massage is much more than relaxing mindfulness. A therapeutic massage can also help you feel better by releasing physical pain.

9. **Dance.** It's okay to dance alone in your kitchen. Or you can dance with a partner or group of friends at a club. Take a few dance lessons to learn the salsa or swing dance, and dance

until you are out of breath. Breathing hard relieves stress by bringing oxygen and endorphins into your system.

10. **Lift weights.** Some local community colleges open their gyms to residents, but you can also get inexpensive weights for easy at-home sessions. One client used full water bottles as weights when he traveled. Regular weight lifting makes you look and feel stronger—a feeling that can carry over into other aspects of your life as well.

CASE IN POINT

Justin was a self-described workaholic, but when he and Jess separated, he found himself struggling with sadness and worries. When I suggested self-care ideas, he was inspired to take up basketball, which he had set aside when he married. This was helpful physically, of course, and it nudged him into social interactions when he joined pickup games at the gym. In addition, he began to take cooking classes during some of his off-duty time. Finally, he visited several churches in his community until he found one where he felt comfortable enough to attend services several times a month.

The separation was still painful for Justin, but he found that these and other self-care practices made him feel that he could handle his emotions. He was more relaxed at home with his three children and enjoyed his time with them. Learning to cook special meals for Meghan, their anorexic daughter, was actually fun for him, especially when she cooked with him. He even had some moments of hopefulness about the unknown future that lay before him.

Spiritual Self-Care Ideas

Spiritual self-care can involve organized religion but isn't limited to it. Ultimately, spirituality is about how you connect to something greater than yourself. You may follow a faith tradition or focus on a personal sense of connection with a higher power, the universe, and so on. Separation and the transition to nesting can make you question your faith, your feeling of safety in the world, your sense of purpose or value. Turning to spiritual self-care is comforting. A spiritual community may provide welcome support in this time of change. Connecting or reconnecting to your spiritual practices may even help bring existential meaning back into your life. Here are a few examples:

1. **Attending a religious service.** Take some time to go to a service or to pray. It can be a faith you've been involved in for years, or a new one you want to try.

2. **Meditate.** The basic idea of meditation is to find a quiet place to sit (or walk) and just focus on your breath. Your mind will certainly wander, but when you notice that you have drifted away from your breath, return your attention to each inhale and exhale. As you focus on this activity, negative feelings or self-critical thoughts will begin releasing their hold on your mind. Start with two minutes each day.

3. **Practice random acts of kindness.** Random acts of kindness are easy to do, and so uplifting. Think about filling someone's expired parking meter or picking up litter along a walking trail. Write a nice note to the waitstaff or chef when you pay your restaurant check.

4. **Pray.** Prayer looks and sounds different to everyone, so simply do it your way. Whether you're invoking a specific deity or just sending good energy out into the universe, praying can help you remember that you're part of a vast universe.

5. **Volunteer.** You can knit caps or make quilts for a local hospital, visit with seniors at a care center, or feed animals at a rescue center. Your generosity will improve someone's day and make you feel good too.

6. **Get your hands dirty.** Tending to plants causes your body to release oxytocin, a feel-good hormone that has also been called the "tend-and-befriend" hormone. You can work in your home garden or care for a few houseplants or bring your green thumb to a community garden. Your off-duty site may feel homier if you bring in some plants too.

7. **Talk with a spiritual adviser.** You can visit with a priest, rabbi, minister, pastor, shaman, life coach, or other spiritual figure to share personal struggles in confidence or ask for advice.

8. **Read a spiritual passage.** You may like to read the Bible or other spiritual texts to nourish your soul and add meaning to your current situation. You might then meditate on the passage you just read.

9. **Explore new religious practices or rituals.** You may like to clear your living space with sage or frankincense or go to a sweat lodge available through a Native American community. There are many purifying rituals in every religion and culture. Let your curiosity be your guide.

10. **Consult an astrologer or a psychic.** If you'd find it helpful, talk to an expert to learn more about yourself and your future. It can be transformative or just interesting.

KEY POINTS TO REMEMBER

- Self-care is necessary for maintaining good health, especially during times of stress.

- Some habits, such as abusing drugs or alcohol, disguise themselves as self-care, but they are actually self-destructive and only make the situation worse.

- Self-care does not necessarily cost money: Most self-care practices are free.

- The four main elements of self-care are mental, physical, emotional, and spiritual.

- Try out different types of self-care to figure out what works for you, and include these things in your regular routine.

CHAPTER 10

What Comes after Nesting?

You know that nesting is temporary, but how do you decide on an actual timeline? When do you begin to think about your next steps? How do you think through those life-changing decisions? What factors should you consider as you contemplate your future, and how do you move from nesting to whatever comes next? This chapter will answer these questions and many others to prepare you for your next transition.

Preparing for Your Next Steps While You Nest

Now that you have worked out your nesting agreement (and perhaps started nesting), you might find that over time your outlook has changed in one way or another from where you started immediately after the decision to separate. On one hand, you might find yourself ready to make the separation more final: Perhaps you are more accepting at this point of the idea of a permanent separation or divorce. You may be feeling more clearheaded now that you have some distance from the stress of your relationship. You may be thinking more concretely about what your future could be like without your spouse. You may have even begun to explore the various legal divorce processes in order to understand the law and what you might expect when it is over. You may be preparing yourself to communicate to your spouse that you are ready to end nesting and finalize your separation.

On the other hand, you may also be considering reconciliation with your spouse, thinking about what that would entail. You may be identifying what it is that you want and need in your relationship and from your partner. You may have begun counseling with your spouse with the goal of determining the future of your marriage.

You may also find that the nesting works so well for your family that you hope to continue it until the children are fully grown and have "left the nest." This isn't common but not unheard of.

When Should You End Nesting?

There's no one right answer to this question. It's a personal decision that you and/or your partner will make. This might happen, for example, if one of you decides to move ahead with divorce or if both of you decide to work toward reconciliation.

Even if you haven't made a final decision, it's kind and respectful to share your thoughts about when to end nesting so you are both on the same page and no one is surprised by what transpires. That's good practice both for practical (if you are thinking about ending the nesting without reconciling, give your spouse at least a few months' notice so that you both can make new living arrangements) and emotional reasons.

ENDING WITH A MILESTONE

Often the nesting ends somewhat naturally when a certain milestone is reached. For example, some parents have nested until a previously nonworking spouse was able to find a job, a child graduated from middle or high school, or until the family home had been sold. Many end the nesting when the legal part of the divorce is finished and you have clarity about where you each stand financially.

You and your spouse may have already identified the milestone event at which time you will end the nesting. Or you may see a milestone or important event on the horizon that tells you nesting could end and it seems right to you.

CASE IN POINT

When Brad and Emma decided to nest, they had agreed to nest at least until William turned nineteen when other social services would step in to help him with housing and other support. Brad and Emma were committed to this plan and milestone because of their shared love for William.

ENDING BECAUSE OF A NEW RELATIONSHIP

If either of you is in a new relationship, it is likely that at some point you will want to pursue it without moving in and out of the house. Nesting often ends when one of you has developed a new committed romantic relationship. Some couples want out of the limbo of "not married and not divorced." This is a sensitive subject and one to approach with care. Use the communication tactics in Chapter 7 to share this news thoughtfully.

CASE IN POINT

Derek and Deb had been nesting for nine months, and it hadn't been an easy time for Deb. Not only was she still very angry and hurt about Derek's affair and ongoing relationship, but he also had triggered her anger when he hired a babysitter to care for the children rather than offering Deb the option to cover for him. She felt devalued and unloved but was determined to protect her children from the conflicts with Derek.

After nine months, Derek told Deb that his girlfriend was feeling insecure about his level of commitment and questioning whether he would ever divorce. So he told Deb he wanted to move in with his girlfriend and end the nesting.

LISTEN TO YOUR GUT

If you have been nesting in order to give yourself time to make a decision about the future of your marriage, be sure to check in with yourself about where you stand now that you've had a break from the daily stresses of your marriage. Perhaps you have used the time to seek therapy and take stock of your marriage, working with or without your spouse. If you are still struggling to see a way forward, a therapist who specializes in discernment counseling can focus on helping you come to a decision about reconciliation or divorce.

Your family and friends may have strong feelings one way or the other about divorce and reconciliation. A word of caution: While their intentions may be loving and supportive, don't allow their opinions to guide your decision. You're the expert on what you can live with in your relationship, and you're the one who will live with the ultimate decision.

The Decision-Making Process

Making the decision to divorce is one of the hardest decisions you will ever have to make. Sometimes, the decision becomes clear quite suddenly. One client called this a "sparkling moment of clarity." When there has been addiction, abuse, or infidelity, for example, the decision may be clear-cut.

Most people, however, face indecision and worry that they'll make the wrong choice. The longer you have been married, the more you have invested in the relationship, and the harder it is to decide to end it. When you have children, the decision can be even more complex and difficult.

At the same time, you may feel as if you are in limbo during nesting. On one hand, you might have gotten the emotional space to consider a life without your spouse. On the other, the lack of conflict with your spouse might remind you of better times. Your emotions shift from hopefulness to despair and back again. This indecision can take a toll on you, your job, your health, and your relationships. It can also be a time of confusion for your children, who may maintain a hope that you and your spouse will reunite.

USING COMMON DECISION-MAKING STRATEGIES

Moving from indecision to decisiveness is possible, no matter how conflicted you feel now. Some people make lists of pros and cons; some people talk to a therapist. Another option is the 10-10-10 method created by Suzy Welch in her bestselling book about making decisions, *10-10-10: A Fast and Powerful Way to Get Unstuck in Love, at Work, and at Home.* She suggests that you consider your options by asking yourself three questions:

- What will be the consequences and how will I feel about this in ten minutes?
- What will be the consequences and how will I feel about this in ten months?
- What will be the consequences and how will I feel about this in ten years?

TAKE YOUR TIME

No matter how you come to your decision, remember that making a big decision in the middle of a crisis is never a good idea. Take the time to get to a safe and stable place emotionally so that your thinking will be rational.

Things to Consider Before Divorcing

As you weigh your options, think about the following factors, which often come into play when a marriage is struggling.

Did You Try Therapy?

Have you and your spouse found a good marital therapist and taken the time to deeply examine your relationship? Many of my clients have told me that they want to "leave no stone unturned." Therapy or counseling doesn't mean one or two sessions, but at least twenty sessions.

If you have worked with a marital therapist, you may feel reassured that you have given the relationship your best effort. If you haven't, you may later regret your decision to divorce. Worse yet, you may carry the same problems of this marriage into your next relationship.

Marital problems will not solve themselves. If one or both of you are unwilling to work on the marriage, to go to marital therapy, or to work on your own issues, there is little hope that the marriage can survive over the long term. Both of you must be willing to work on the issues, and even then, despite sincere efforts, the marriage may not be repaired.

Have You Tried to Improve Your Communication?

One of the most common reasons for divorce that I have heard is the lack of communication or poor communication. Your communication may have improved during the nesting period, perhaps due to the lack of conflict and/or your focus on the tips suggested in Chapter 7. Listening to your spouse and expressing yourself respectfully keeps a cordial relationship alive. Investing in developing good listening and communication skills will allow your relationship to improve. Even if you go on to divorce, good communication through the divorce and over the long term will benefit you both, as well as your children.

Are You Holding On to Past Arguments?

The hurt caused by conflict may last for years. If you or your spouse keeps bringing the accumulating hurts of the past into the arguments ("you always…you never…"), it will be hard to move on and find peace.

Can You Both Compromise?

Are you and your spouse able to work out compromises when you disagree? Can you apologize and repair when necessary? Are you able to forgive?

If not, the relationship can deteriorate into a power struggle or a battle for control. Alternatively, one of you may simply resign and give up. Sometimes you know the marriage is over when you stop arguing. You just do not care anymore.

Have You Addressed Fraught Topics?

Marriages often break down over differences of opinion regarding money, sex, children (parenting), or religion. I've seen all of these in my practice. If these are the issues you face in your relationship, have you worked on them with the help of an expert? If you have had those difficult conversations, and there is no improvement, you may be satisfied that you have done all you can possibly do to save your marriage.

Have You Dealt with Intimacy Issues?

If you feel that there's no longer any intimacy in your relationship, and you don't talk about it, chances are good that you and your spouse will drift apart. Intimacy is about sex, affection, and a deep sense of connection, feeling valued, loved, and understood. If these needs are not being met and haven't been addressed, you or your spouse may seek to find other ways to meet those needs, and the relationship will wither and die. If you don't listen and talk with your spouse, one or both of you may find someone else who does.

Can You Reconnect with Each Other?

Have you felt like you and your spouse have been drifting apart, or that you have nothing in common anymore, nothing to talk about and no shared interests?

Perhaps you have focused on your children and ignored your spouse's needs. Or you may feel that you are no longer a priority for your spouse, or perhaps you're feeling overly controlled by your spouse. You may be fantasizing about what it would be like to be single. Reconnecting in a meaningful way will be key to any reconciliation.

Is Either of You Keeping Secrets?

If you or your spouse is keeping secrets about money or other relationships, it's a big warning sign that the marriage needs help. If you have developed an addiction to gambling, shopping, or drugs, and have tried to hide this from your spouse, this is a further indication of big problems that need to be resolved. You'll need to disclose all of your financial information, including any losses, during your divorce. If either of you is fantasizing about another person or having an emotional or physical affair, you'll need to do a lot of work to repair the marriage, but only if you both want to and are willing to do so.

ASSESS WHAT NESTING HAS CLARIFIED FOR YOU

These issues may have drawn you to the idea of nesting in order to sort out your feelings and desires for your marriage. If so, what (if anything) has changed in your relationship during the nesting period? Have there been improvements in any of the issues? How long do you think you could live in the marriage the way that it is now if nothing changes? There is no easy way to come to this difficult decision, but considering these factors will allow you to feel like you've exhausted all of your options before moving to divorce.

Specific Steps to Divorce

Either or both of you can make the decision to divorce. If your spouse makes it, the decision will be out of your hands. It takes two people to work on reconciliation, but it only takes one person to start a divorce. If your spouse decides to divorce, the divorce will happen, even if you oppose the idea. All states in the United States have some form of no-fault divorce now, which means that anyone can get a divorce without showing any wrongdoing by the other spouse.

You might be the one to lead the decision to divorce. If so, set up a time to talk with your spouse. You'll need to explain your intentions and ask him or her to work with you to make a plan. This could be a difficult conversation if your partner does not want the divorce. Be gentle and compassionate when you express your intentions.

No matter how you come to the decision to divorce, here's how to proceed:

1. Discuss the next steps with your spouse. Will you begin the legal process now or wait for a while?

2. Decide when the nesting will end. You may want to give yourselves some time to reorganize your living situation.

3. Decide how your living situation will change—will one or both of you find a new residence?

4. Decide when to tell the children. Plan what you will say together. Be prepared to explain what will change and what will stay the same. Reassure them by modeling cooperation with your spouse. Protect them from the details of the legal process, settlement issues, and financial concerns.

5. Discuss whether you will be able to work together with a mediator or collaborative divorce attorneys. Do some research about the various divorce process options in your area. Remember that the default in most states is litigation; you must *choose* mediation or collaborative divorce. Decide whether you will consult with attorneys now, separately or together.

6. Recommit to a transparent and amicable process and to continue a healthy co-parenting relationship.

CASE IN POINT

Allie and Jack nested for about a year and a half before moving ahead with their divorce. Allie wasn't happy about Jack's decision to get a divorce, but the nesting period gave her the time to accept his decision. She became more independent and eventually began to feel less sad and anxious. She developed new culinary skills during her off-duty time and began to sell her homemade baked goods to local shops. She joined a hiking group and made time to see friends and family.

Continuing to talk with each other about how to ease the transition from nesting to two homes, Allie and Jack shared information regularly about the children and gave each other space to parent the children in their own styles. As her trust in Jack's solo parenting developed, Allie's worries about the children decreased.

When Jack suggested that they begin the actual process of divorce, Allie was ready to start. They chose a collaborative divorce, which gave them each professional support. The collaborative process put them in control of all the decisions they would make to settle their property, financial, and parenting issues.

Issues to Think about Before Reconciling

About 13 percent of separated couples decide to reconcile. Perhaps the passage of time and the respite has changed your attitude too. If you've continued individual therapy or couple's work during the nesting, you may feel differently about your partner or your marriage. Here are some things to consider when you are contemplating a reconciliation.

WHAT ARE YOUR MOTIVES?

Think about *why* you are considering reconciliation. Is it because you still love your spouse, or are you afraid to be the one to make the decision to divorce? Are you frightened of the unknown future, bored, or lonely? Perhaps you feel you have not done enough to save your marriage.

WHAT'S CHANGED SINCE YOU SEPARATED?

What has changed since you started nesting? Have the problems that led to your separation been addressed or resolved (anger, addiction, affair, etc.)? Are you both willing to get help?

IS THE DECISION COMING FROM YOU?

Don't allow your stress, fear, or guilt make your decision. Don't give in to pressure from family or friends. Base your decision on information and a clear understanding of what reconciliation would look like for you and your spouse. Take all the time you need to think about it.

ARE YOU AND YOUR PARTNER ON THE SAME PAGE?

If you want to consider reconciliation, schedule a time to talk with your spouse to see if he or she agrees. Reconciling will only work if you *both* agree. Then discuss what you will do to ensure the success of your decision. Are you both willing to have difficult conversations to resolve the issues that led you to your decision to nest? Are you both able to make a commitment to doing the work to heal past hurts, betrayals, and resentments? Are you both committed to doing the work to repair and revive your marriage? Can you forgive? Can you apologize?

HAVE YOU PLANNED HOW TO PROCEED?

If you both decide to reconcile, discuss the steps and pacing of your reconciliation. You may continue to nest for a while and plan regular weekly dates and therapy. Take your time, because repairing a relationship is hard work and needs time. You didn't get here overnight, and repairing a marriage doesn't happen overnight either.

CASE IN POINT

You may recall Phillip and Fran from Chapter 2. They developed a nesting arrangement to support Fran's sobriety and hoped to reconcile. They still loved each other, but Fran's drinking threatened their marriage. To assure his wife of the seriousness of his intention, Phillip completed all the divorce papers in case Fran relapsed again. Fran's continued sobriety was supported by their nesting agreement, and they decided to reconcile. When I last heard from them, their marriage was thriving.

Your Next Steps to Reconciliation

If you want to consider reconciliation, here's how to proceed:

1. Set up a time to meet with your spouse. Explain your desire to work toward reconciliation, and ask whether he or she will consider this. If so, ask to work on a plan together.

2. Commit to a certain amount of time to explore reconciliation. Give yourself plenty of time. For example, agree to six months of regular weekly counseling, plus twice-a-week "dates" to get to know each other again.

3. Discuss how you'll begin the process. Talk about what went wrong and how to change or fix those things. Be specific about patterns, behaviors, and dynamics that you will each change. Commit to making changes yourself based on feedback from your spouse and your counselor, if you have one.

4. Talk openly and honestly about your hopes, goals, wants, needs, and expectations. Share your vision of what your mar-

riage will look like and what you will each do to achieve that vision. Work together to understand each other's wants and needs to see if they are compatible. Consider where you might compromise.

5. When will you resume sexual relations? Many couples have a very hard time talking about sex, even though it is critical to do so. Consider discussing the resumption of sexual relations with your marital therapist, particularly if this was one of the issues that led to your separation. In some marriages, sex might have been one of the things that worked best in the relationship. In this case, talk openly together about when you will each be ready to resume your sexual life.

6. Review your financial arrangement. If you separated your finances during the nesting, do you want to keep things that way for now? Discuss how this will look when you reconcile— that is, who will be responsible for which expenses? You may seek the help of your CPA if you decide to keep your finances separate or to merge your finances again. If there were financial problems during the marriage (overspending, credit card debt, or different values about money), be sure to address them now.

7. Discuss your nesting agreement. Keeping things stable for your children during this time will help the two of you focus on your relationship. What, if anything, will you change in your nesting agreement? For example, will you start weekly family dinners at some point? Again, don't rush. It probably took years to get to where your marriage is now, and it will take time to change course. Give yourself the time to reconnect with each other in deep and meaningful ways. Don't move back in together immediately, in order to protect your

children from another possible breakup if the reconciliation doesn't work out.

8. When will you inform friends and family? Other than very close family or friends, it's wise to wait until you've spoken with your children and you are completely sure that the reconciliation will last before spreading the word.

Tips for Helping Your Children Transition Away from Nesting

You and your spouse have made some important and difficult decisions about your next steps. Whether you decide to divorce or reconcile, a smooth transition is vital for your children. Here are some steps:

1. Decide where you each will live. If you will be living in separate homes, confirm those arrangements. If one of you will be staying in the family home, give the other time to find a new long-term residence. If you'll begin to live together again, decide whether you will remain in the present home.

2. If you plan to divorce, discuss the schedule. Will you keep the current nesting schedule? Will you change it based on the new circumstances?

3. Review your parenting plan. You'll probably need to update it with some adjustments and additions, so set aside some time to review it carefully, perhaps with the help of a therapist who specializes in child development and divorce.

4. Meet to plan how and when you will tell your children about your decisions. You should tell them together, if possible, and before they hear it from someone else.

5. If you are moving ahead with a divorce, explain to your children what will change. If they will be starting to move back and forth between your two homes, give them concrete information, like when it will start and where their new home will be. Tell them, "We are still one family, under two roofs." Show them the new home and let them help create their own spaces. They may want to bring special items from the nesting home to the new home.

6. Debrief your nesting experience. If your children are teens, they may want to debrief as well, so invite their feedback. One of the families I interviewed, described in the following appendix, said that they never discussed the nesting and later regretted that. Share appreciations with each other about what worked, and what went well. If you are divorcing, this sets the tone for a more respectful and amicable divorce.

CONSIDER A RITUAL TO MARK THE CHANGE

I often help families create a ritual or rite of passage to mark the transition from nesting to what comes next. Monza Naff, PhD, wrote a book of such rituals. *Must We Say We Did Not Love?* has inspired many divorcing parents to create their own rituals. In one example, the parents gave each of their children necklaces that held a key to both Mom's and Dad's houses.

Divorce is a rite of passage, but one that is often seen in our culture as a "failure" and therefore rarely honored. Yes, a divorce is the end of a relationship, but it's also the birth of something new. A divorce ritual is a way of marking the transition in a more positive way that truly supports family values.

KEY POINTS TO REMEMBER

- Take as much time as you need to make your decision to reconcile or divorce. Don't let your emotions push you into an impulsive decision.

- Think through what worked and didn't work in your marriage, and whether it can be repaired. Think about whether you'll feel good about the decision in ten minutes, ten months, and ten years.

- Discuss your thoughts or decision with your spouse and plan your next steps. Perhaps your spouse has also made a decision to divorce or to try to reconcile.

- It takes two of you to reconcile and only one to divorce.

- Plan your next steps thoughtfully, and if you are going to divorce, aim for a mutual consent process such as mediation or collaborative divorce. Stay out of court if you can.

- Prepare your children for the transition from nesting to what comes next.

Appendix:
One Family's Story

In the Introduction of this book, I asked you to consider the story you would like your children to tell of their parents' divorce. Nesting will be a part of their story. In this appendix, you will hear from a family of five who nested for more than six years! That may be a longer period of time than most, but their story is valuable because it captures each person's views. While each family member tells a different story of the nesting period and divorce, all agree that nesting helped them adjust and adapt to the changes in the family.

Throughout this book, I've tracked a number of couples and families to illustrate various nesting experiences. Now let's hear directly from all the members of one family, each of whom has her or his own subjective point of view. As you read the comments from Helen's family, you will feel the authenticity of each perspective even when they don't agree. All the names and certain details have been changed to protect their confidentiality.

HELEN

My husband and I decided to separate in 1983. We'd never heard of nesting, but we wanted the process to be as stable, amicable, and painless as possible for our kids. We agreed to focus on our children, despite our emotional stress. They were thirteen, fifteen, and seventeen. We planned to nest 'til our youngest was out of high school, and we did.

We didn't really explain nesting to the kids. That was probably a mistake, but we didn't know better. One day we were in the car and we just tossed it out from the front seat, "We are getting a divorce," and they were shocked. I wish we'd found a better way to tell them. Our families and friends were mostly supportive of the nesting, though they probably didn't like that we were divorcing.

It was a really hard time. I'd forget stuff, I'd mess up the schedule, and I felt conflicted and lost. I felt what it was like to be a kid, always forgetting my stuff at one place or another. I'm glad our kids didn't have to do that. I should have gone to counseling; I needed more support. I didn't see as much of my friends because I felt so ashamed. I felt like I should have worked harder at the marriage. I've mostly forgiven myself by now.

We never had a formal "nesting agreement," but our most important rule was to keep things as normal as possible. We wrote up a family contract that we called a "Fairness Contract." Even the kids signed it. It said that we each needed to do whatever was necessary to love and respect each other, work together, and support each other.

One rule was to never have overnight visitors, and we never violated that one. We also agreed to keep a tidy home. We never talked about privacy or private spaces in the home, but the privacy issue is important. You need to trust the other person will respect your privacy.

We left each other notes at the house or met for lunch to talk about how things were going. We had to talk about the schedule regularly because his work schedule varied. We also saw each other at sports games and holidays, and we even took family trips together. We got along so much better after we separated.

Now when I hear people are nesting, I hope they get support and pay attention to their own feelings. I wish I'd had a support group and someone to help me figure out my finances. Thankfully, we didn't argue about money, and we had similar parenting values. We were good co-parents most of the time because we trusted each other.

It takes work, but nesting's ideal for kids. Our kids did hold out hope that we'd get back together. I have wondered if nesting prolonged their adjustment to the reality of our divorce. However, we'd do it all again if we turned back the clock. My kids are doing great now. I wonder what they remember and whether they think it was a good experience.

MAX

I don't see how our nesting could have been any better. Helen and I weren't on the same page about many things, but we were on the same page regarding parenting. I don't think we actually discussed this, but we had an agreement to put the kids first. We didn't want them to go back and forth, especially since we weren't sure about whether we would stay together or not. (When we started nesting, we didn't know we were going to divorce.) It just made sense to us to keep things stable in the meantime. At some point, I decided that we weren't going to continue as a married couple and wanted to start to date. We agreed to continue to nest.

We worked out the money issues of nesting without conflict. She didn't have an income at that time because she was in school. We decided to sell our house before we nested so that she could have some money and I could buy a smaller house. The new house, my house, is where we nested. She got half of the money and paid for all her own expenses. I realized I was getting a break because I didn't have to pay her alimony. It seemed like a fair deal then and it still does. When we severed our financial ties, she was independent and became self-sufficient.

While we were nesting, we were cordial with each other. We were careful with each other's feelings. We still did some of the holidays together, like Christmas. There were also some harder times, but I still have a good relationship with her family, and I am glad about that. In the past few years, we have also shared events with our kids, grandchildren, and with the whole family, and these social events have gotten easier over time. Now that we have grandchildren, I think it is great that we can all get together, laugh, and get along.

I know that at first the kids were disappointed and didn't like the idea that we were separating. I wasn't aware that they were having any problems with the nesting. I didn't see any signs that they were suffering. We all just had the attitude of "Let's just press on." Maybe they shared more with their mom, and if Helen suggested something about the kids, I would generally go along with it. Usually, I thought she saw things I didn't see and her ideas were good ones. I guess you'd call that trust.

Now, looking back, I think it must have been fine because the kids all seem happy and successful in their own lives today. They all seem to have come through unscathed; all of them have families and jobs. I feel good about it. Actually, I have never spoken with them about what they remember, what they thought. I would be curious to hear what they have to say about it.

TIFFANY

I remember when our parents told us they were divorcing. We were in the car, and it was confusing and upsetting. But we knew our parents weren't happy. We saw their bickering, and it was a relief when they separated and that stopped.

When the nesting started, Mom had been going to grad school already, so we'd gotten used to her not being home all the time. But Dad started doing more with us, and that was really nice.

I was lonely, to be honest. It didn't feel like a family anymore. I was fifteen, and it felt like I was supposed to be separating from my parents, but they were separating from us. We were never a family that talked about our feelings, but I wish I could have talked to my siblings. I would just go into my room and cry, feeling sad and lonely. We still have never talked about it. I think we could have done a lot better supporting each other, sharing our feelings. I think we all just kind of detached.

I know our parents nested because they thought it would be the least disruptive for us. Nesting did provide stability for us. We woke up in our own beds every day. It would have been terrible to have to pick a parent to live with. Looking back, divorce is always hard for kids, and maybe the nesting made it a little easier. I wish I had told my parents how sad I was, and that I needed help, but we just didn't share feelings. I realize they were trying to shelter us from the divorce stuff, but I wish I had understood more what was going on.

We kids became more independent after the nesting started, but our basic needs were definitely met. Someone always came home to make dinner for us. One or both of my parents would always be there for concerts or games, and we still did family stuff, like camping, and we still had fun. I remember one time when both my parents helped me with homework, and how nice that was. Even though we still did things together as a family, and we liked doing that, I felt an unspoken tension between my parents.

I imagine my younger brother had the hardest time of all because he was home alone for three years after my sister and I had gone off to college.

I don't really know if it would have been better or worse if they hadn't nested. Divorce is just always hard for kids. I have been married for many years and would be willing to put up with anything to be with my children full time. Nesting was probably an easier way to experience divorce as a kid. It could have been so much worse. They went through these crazy nesting gymnastics so we wouldn't have to move around. I am glad that they tried to make it easier for us, but I do wish our family had talked more, especially about feelings. I hope other families get their kids to open up and if they need help, that they get it.

JASON

I was just starting junior high when things changed. I didn't want to believe they were actually separating. They didn't say they were nesting or divorcing, but eventually I figured it out. I think I just accepted it.

My life didn't change a lot at first. I stayed at the same school. I was pretty self-absorbed, and I just kept doing what I had been doing: school, sports, friends. The biggest change was I didn't see as much of Mom and I saw a lot more of Dad. Dad was more engaged when they nested than he had been before. Also, and I think this helped, they always spoke highly of each other.

I don't remember my parents ever asking us about how we were doing. If I wanted to talk to someone, I would go to my sisters. I didn't talk to anyone else about our home life. I must have been difficult because I didn't talk much. But I was a super-happy kid growing up. I just didn't want to talk to anyone.

I know my parents tried hard, but I missed my mom. I didn't have any negative feelings toward her; I just missed her. When we were nesting, the schedule changed all the time, which was hard. Before the nesting, it seemed like there was always one or both parents at home. When they were nesting, it seemed like I spent more time alone at home than kids with two parents at home.

The hardest part was when my sisters went to college. When it was just me and Dad. I was a normal, moody teenager, and I don't think it was because of their divorce.

I'm actually divorced now myself. I think what's different about my divorce is that we have a consistent schedule with who's watching the kids. We share the parenting and communicate pretty well. Maybe I was able to have a good divorce because my parents worked so hard to have an easier divorce.

It's hard to say how the nesting affected me because the nesting, the move, Mom in school, and the divorce all came together. It's hard to separate the nesting from everything else. But I think the nesting, and my parents' respectful relationship, made it all easier. Now I'm very close to both of my parents even though I don't see them as much as I used to because I live so far away.

My advice to anyone thinking about nesting is to be as consistent as possible in the schedule. Cherish every moment with your kids and try not to let them know how unhappy you are. Happier parents make happier kids, I think. Keep your kids as your number one priority. Give them affection and tell them you love them all the time, but don't make them your best friend. You're still the parent. Make things as easy as possible and make the transitions easy. That's what I learned from my parents' nesting and what I am doing now with my ex and my kids.

What my parents did by nesting was fantastic. It was probably hard for them to decide to divorce. They did their best to make it easier for us, and now I can say I really appreciate that.

MOLLY

My parents started nesting when I was a junior in high school. I think they explained what they were doing, but I don't remember. I was very surprised when they said they were divorcing. I didn't know anything was wrong. We didn't see it coming.

Not a lot changed, except I had to take on a lot more responsibility. I was annoyed because I had to drive my siblings around sometimes. That was the biggest change. I stayed in the same school, the same job, my same car, my same friends, everything. We always had to do chores and that stayed the same. We always had family dinners, but now we had them with whichever parent was there. That was important.

Maybe there was less tension in the house. Both my parents were as engaged with me as they had been before. They were great about never saying bad things about each other. I actually thought it was great because I got to spend time with each parent without having to move from place to place. I still had a good relationship with them both.

I think nesting is amazing for kids. I don't know if I could nest, because it is so hard for the parents. I feel grateful to my parents because it would have been traumatic if we had to shuffle back and forth. Now I realize how hard it must have been for them. They took on the burden of all the logistics and moving back and forth.

We sibs didn't talk to each other about it. I don't remember my parents checking in to see how I was doing either.

I think I changed because of the nesting. I am more open-minded now. I have been married twenty-five years, and if we had got divorced, I might have considered nesting so the kids could have shared time with each of us. I am glad that they are grown now and I don't have to make that decision! It was so good for us kids. The divorce didn't ruin my childhood.

I'd tell parents that nesting is an amazing thing to do for the kids. I would say to go ahead and do it, even though I am not even sure I would have!

I would also say, "Everyone, please get family therapy, even if you think you don't need it!" I never talked about my feelings back then, and I am just starting to sort out my feelings now. I probably would have resisted it, but I think it would have been beneficial. I'd tell kids to appreciate that their parents were doing that for them. I'd say, "You're going to be okay."

I am curious to hear what the rest of my family said about our nesting. Maybe I will set up a family therapy session so we can share.

I feel very lucky; I'm close to both of my parents, and they seem happy. If they had to go their separate ways, they did it in a way that they carried the entire burden so we kids could have a normal life.

Afterword

We have come to the conclusion of our journey together. Now that you have decided on your next steps and expressed appreciation to each other for the success of the nesting, you're ready to move on. My hope is that, whether you reconcile or divorce, a positive nesting experience will help you make a smooth transition to the next chapter of your life. The skills you have learned in this book and experienced as you nested will serve you well, no matter what the future holds for you.

As you move forward, remember to use your favorite self-care strategies. Pay attention to your emotions, and seek support when you need it. Stay focused on the future, on your strengths and successes, and remember that every problem has a solution. You just need to look for it and you will find it.

I hope that your children will thrive and that the story they will tell of this time in their lives will express the peace, security, and love that you have given them.

Additional Resources

CHAPTER 3: Developing a Co-Parenting Plan

Parents have different parenting styles. For more information about best practices for co-parenting, this website is a useful resource: *www.helpguide.org/articles/parenting-family/co-parenting-tips-for-divorced-parents.htm/.*

A number of articles about parenting at each stage of child development: *https://centerforparentingeducation.org/library-of-articles/.*

There are various parenting plan worksheets on the Internet. I find this one developed by Gary Direnfeld, MSW, RSW, to be the most straightforward, and it is modifiable to fit your family's situation: *www.yoursocialworker.com/s-articles/Parenting_plan.pdf.*

Helpful suggestions for building single-parenting skills: *www.liveabout.com/how-to-be-a-better-parent-2997896.*

This article helps reframe the single-parenting role by exploring its benefits: *www.parents.com/parenting/dynamics/single-parenting/benefits-to-being-a-single-parent/.*

CHAPTER 6: Talking to Your Kids (and Others) about Nesting

Therapists have adapted and shared this list with parents who are going through separation or divorce. The list helps parents understand their children's experiences and needs: "13 Things Kids Want Parents to Know," by Isolina Ricci, PhD. Excerpted from "Divorce from the Kids' Point of View." *NCFR Report*, December 2007.

CHAPTER 7: Sharing Information While Nesting

Karla McLaren. *The Language of Emotions: What Your Feelings Are Trying to Tell You.* Louisville, Colorado: Sounds True, 2010. You can download a free emotional vocabulary list here: *https://karlamclaren.com/wp-content/uploads/2016/05/Emotional-Vocabulary-List-Color.pdf.*

Another useful "Feelings and Emotions Vocabulary Word List": *www .enchantedlearning.com/wordlist/emotions.shtml.*

If you struggle with self-criticism or guilt, this handout will be helpful: *www.tasha-harmon.com/pdf/Taming_Your_Inner_Critic_Handout.pdf.*

This scale is designed to give you the ability to self-evaluate the effects of the recent changes you have experienced. This is important because research has shown that stress affects your immune system and is a predictor of illness. The higher your score, the more important it is that you reduce your stress through self-care practices and counseling:
Thomas H. Holmes and Richard Rahe. "The Social Readjustment Rating Scale." *Journal of Psychosomatic Research* 11, no. 2 (1967). *www.mindtools .com/pages/article/newTCS_82.htm.*

This link takes you to the original stress inventory developed by Holmes and Rahe. Included is a guide to meditation and other self-care activities: *www.talent.wisc.edu/Home/Portals/0/OPC/2009/Letting%20Go%20of%20 Stress.pdf.*

Google Calendar is an example of a free and very useful shared calendar. Some families also have a shared calendar that the children can access to track the time-sharing schedule.

Our Family Wizard is another co-parenting app, and scheduling and communication tool, and paid by subscription. It's much more comprehensive than a shared calendar: *www.ourfamilywizard.com/.*

A reference sheet detailing a communication tool that reduces conflict by controlling provocative communications: Bill Eddy. "How to Give a BIFF Response." High Conflict Institute, 2007. *www.scmediation.org/wp-content/ uploads/2016/11/BIFF-Article.2014final.pdf.*

CHAPTER 9: Taking Care of Yourself

"1,132 Positive Affirmations: Your Daily List of Simple Mantras": *www.developgoodhabits.com/positive-affirmations/.*

"39 Best Adult Coloring Books for Relaxing & Stress Relief": *www.developgoodhabits.com/adult-coloring-books/.*

Another downloadable, printable list of self-care ideas: *https://kecsac.eku.edu/ sites/kecsac.eku.edu/files/files/Trauma%20Informed%20Care%20Self-Care%20Activities%20Handout.pdf.*

CHAPTER 10: What Comes after Nesting?

Discernment counseling is a type of brief couples therapy designed for couples who are uncertain whether they want to continue their relationship. It can also be used in cases where one partner wants to end the relationship while the other hopes to preserve it. This type of therapy aims to help partners consider all options before they make the decision to work on or terminate a relationship. Couples who are considering breaking up or getting a divorce but do not know if ending the relationship is the right decision for them may find it helpful to consider their options, and the potential outcomes of these options, with a therapist who practices discernment counseling. For more information, see *www.goodtherapy.org.*

As you consider reconciliation or divorce, look carefully at the history of your relationship. John Gottman, PhD, attributes the breakdown of relationships to the "Four Horsemen of the Apocalypse": criticism, stonewalling (emotional shutdown), defensiveness, and contempt. By the time contempt has seeped into your marriage, it probably is not salvageable. Are you feeling contemptuous of your partner? Is either of you rolling your eyes at the other—a sure sign of contempt? If you are considering reconciliation, Gottman's book is a valuable resource to support the success of your efforts: John Gottman. *The Seven Principles for Making Marriage Work: A Practical Guide from the Country's Foremost Relationship Expert.* New York: Harmony Books, 1999.

A model for evaluating choices and making decisions: Suzy Welch. *10-10-10: A Life-Transforming Idea.* New York: Scribner, 2009.

A new way of normalizing divorce and the transition from one to two homes: Monza Naff. *Must We Say We Did Not Love?* Voices of Integrity, 2016. *www.psychologytoday.com/us/blog/better-divorce/201906/must-we-say-we-did-not-love.*

Further Reading

Ahrons, Constance. *The Good Divorce*. New York: HarperCollins Publishers, 1998.

Bonkowski, Sara. *Tots Are Non-Divorceable: A Workbook for Parents and Their Children*. Chicago: ACTA Publications, 1998.

Burns, Cherie. *Step-Motherhood: How to Survive Without Feeling Frustrated, Left Out or Wicked*. New York: Three Rivers Press, 2001.

Ellis, Carolyn B. *The 7 Pitfalls of Single Parenting: What to Avoid to Help Your Children Thrive after Divorce*. Bloomington, Indiana: iUniverse, 2012.

Emery, Robert E. *The Truth about Children and Divorce: Dealing with the Emotions so You and Your Children Can Thrive*. New York: Plume, 2006.

Gadoua, Susan Pease. *Stronger Day by Day: Reflections for Healing and Rebuilding after Divorce*. Oakland, California: New Harbinger Publications, 2010.

Hannibal, Mary Ellen. *Good Parenting Through Your Divorce*. New York: Marlowe and Company, 2006.

Kalter, Neil. *Growing Up with Divorce: Helping Your Child Avoid Immediate and Later Emotional Problems*. New York: Free Press, 1990.

Lieberman, Alicia F. *The Emotional Life of the Toddler*. New York: Free Press, 2017. (This is an approachable description of how toddlers experience the world. Chapters on the experience of toddlers after a separation/divorce.)

Marston, Stephanie. *The Divorced Parent: Success Strategies for Raising Your Children after Separation*. New York: Morrow, 1994.

Massimo, Mathew, and Sofia Price. *Stepparenting: Becoming a Stepparent: A Blended Family Guide to Parenting, Raising Children, Family Relationships and Step Families*. CreateSpace Independent Publishing Platform, 2015.

McBride, Jean. *Talking to Children about Divorce: A Parent's Guide to Healthy Communication at Each Stage of Divorce*. Berkeley, California: Althea Press, 2016.

Neuman, Gary M. *Helping Your Kids Cope with Divorce the Sandcastles Way.* New York: Random House, 1999.

Oddenino, Michael, and Jeff Carter. *Putting Kids First: Walking Away from a Marriage Without Walking Over the Kids.* Salt Lake City: Family Connections, 1995.

Ricci, Isolina. *Mom's House, Dad's House: Making Two Homes for Your Child.* New York: Fireside, 1997.

Ricci, Isolina. *Mom's House, Dad's House for Kids.* New York: Fireside, 2006.

Schneider, Meg, and Joan Zuckerberg. *Difficult Questions Kids Ask (and Are Too Afraid to Ask) about Divorce.* New York: Simon & Schuster, 1996.

Siegel, Daniel J., and Tina Payne Bryson. *The Whole-Brain Child: 12 Revolutionary Strategies to Nurture Your Child's Developing Mind.* New York: Delacorte, 2012. (This is a wonderfully practical parenting book that is based on neuroscience.)

Wolfelt, Alan D., and Raelynn Maloney. *Healing a Child's Heart after Divorce: 100 Practical Ideas for Families, Friends and Caregivers.* Fort Collins, Colorado: Companion Press, 2011.

PRESCHOOL: Four- to Six-Year-Olds

Abercrombie, Barbara. *Charlie Anderson.* New York: Simon & Schuster, 1995.

Best, Cari. *Taxi! Taxi!* New York: Little, Brown, 2000. (Tina, a school-aged daughter of divorced parents, looks forward to the Sunday afternoons she spends with her Papi, driver of the most yellow taxi in New York City. Each Sunday, Tina and Papi drive to the country to tend their flower and vegetable garden and to enjoy quiet times in each other's company. Spanish words and phrases are sprinkled throughout this realistic picture of life in a bilingual, divorced family.)

Brown, Laurie Krasny and Marc Brown. *Dinosaurs Divorce: A Guide for Changing Families.* New York: Little, Brown, 1988.

Cain, Barbara S. *Double-Dip Feelings: Stories to Help Children Understand Emotions.* Washington, DC: Magination Press, 2001.

Caines, Jeannette. *Daddy.* New York: Harper and Row, 1977. (Child visits father and stepmother each Saturday. African-American stepfamily.)

Christiansen, C.B. *My Mother's House, My Father's House*. New York: Atheneum/Macmillan, 1995.

Helmering, Doris Wild. *I Have Two Families*. Nashville, Tennessee: Abingdon Press, 1981.

Hoffman, Mary. *Boundless Grace*. New York: Puffin Books, 2000. (African-American girl goes to Africa to visit her father.)

Lansky, Vicki. *It's Not Your Fault, Koko Bear: A Read-Together Book for Parents & Young Children During Divorce*. Minnetonka, Minnesota: Book Peddlers, 1998. (Available in English and Spanish.)

Moore-Mallinos, Jennifer. *Daddy's Getting Married*. New York: Barron's, 2006.

Ransom, Jeanie Franz. *I Don't Want to Talk about It*. Washington, DC: Magination Press, 2000.

Willhoite, Michael. *Daddy's Roommate*. New York: Alyson Publications, 1994. (A young child discusses his father's new living situation, in which the father and his gay roommate share eating, doing chores, playing, loving, and living.)

Wyeth, Sharon Dennis. *Always My Dad*. New York: Alfred A. Knopf, 1995. (A father whose visits are unpredictable but treasured reminds his family that, no matter where he is, he's always Dad. Beautiful illustrations of an African-American family. Ages four to eight.)

ELEMENTARY SCHOOL: Seven- to Nine-Year-Olds

Caseley, Judith. *Priscilla Twice*. New York: Greenwillow Books, 1995. (A story of a girl who feels split in half. It helps her understand in reassuring and even humorous ways that there is more than one kind of family.)

Cleary, Beverly, and Paul O. Zelinsky. *Dear Mr. Henshaw*. New York: HarperCollins Publishers, 2000. (An award-winning book about a ten-year-old boy who writes letters to an unmet hero describing how he misses his father. Also available in Spanish.)

Cruise, Robin. *The Top-Secret Journal of Fiona Claire Jardin*. San Diego: Harcourt, 1998.

Johnston, Janet R., Karen Breunig, Carla Garrity, and Mitchell Baris. *Through the Eyes of Children: Healing Stories for Children of Divorce*. New York: Free Press, 1997.

Jong, Erica. *Megan's Two Houses*. Beverly Hills, California: Dove Kids, 1996. (Struggling with the many problems faced by children of divorced families, eight-year-old Megan tries to adjust to having two rooms, two pets, two sets of possessions, and two potential stepparents.)

Karst, Patrice. *The Invisible String*. New York: Little, Brown, 2018.

Menendez-Aponte, Emily. *When Mom and Dad Divorce: A Kid's Resource*. St. Meinrad, Indiana: Abbey Press, 2014.

Park, Barbara. *Don't Make Me Smile*. New York: Random House, 2002. (An eleven-year-old boy feels his life will never be the same again after his parents' divorce; people try to cheer him up to no avail. He goes for professional counseling. Ages eight to twelve.)

Paulsen, Gary. *Hatchet*. London: Macmillan Children's Books, 2017. (In Spanish: *El Hacha*. After a plane crash, thirteen-year-old Brian spends fifty-four days in the wilderness, learning to survive with only the aid of a hatchet given to him by his mother, and also learning to survive his parents' divorce.)

Pickhardt, Carl E. *The Case of the Scary Divorce*. Washington, DC: Imagination Press, 1997. (A ten-year-old boy meets the mysterious "Professor Jackson Skye: Helping Investigator" who enlists his aid in solving eight cases, each dealing with a problem he himself is experiencing during his parents' divorce. Ages nine to twelve.)

Rubin, Judith Aron. *My Mom and Dad Don't Live Together Anymore*. Washington, DC: Imagination Press, 2002.

Schab, Lisa. *The Divorce Workbook for Children: Help for Kids to Overcome Difficult Family Changes & Grow Up Happy*. Oakland, California: New Harbinger Publications, 2008.

Stinson, Kathy. *Mom and Dad Don't Live Together Anymore*. Toronto, Ontario, Canada: Annick Press, 2007.

Tax, Meredith. *Families*. New York: Little, Brown, 2013. (This book illustrates that there are all kinds of families, and "The main thing isn't where they live or how big they are…it's how much they love each other." This book normalizes differences between many types of families and is recommended for children who feel stigmatized by coming from a divorced family. It is culturally sensitive.)

PRETEEN AND TEENAGE

Blume, Judy. *It's Not the End of the World*. New York: Dell, 1986. (This is the story of how a girl and her siblings react to their parents' separation. Karen is concerned about how the family will manage financially and who will take care of them. She tries to get her parents to reconcile. Her six-year-old sister develops fears of the dark and of being left alone. Her fourteen-year-old brother runs away for a few days. Karen meets another girl whose parents are divorced, and learns some new ways of coping from her.)

Danziger, Paula. *The Divorce Express*. New York: Puffin Books, 2014. (A fourteen-year-old girl named Phoebe lives in a joint parenting situation. Problems arise when her mom plans to marry. After Phoebe's parents' divorce, she has to travel every Sunday to see her dad. Just when she thinks she has a handle on it all, her mom makes a decision that will change everything again. Ages twelve to fifteen.)

Evans, Marla D. *This Is Me and My Two Families*. Washington, DC: Magination Press, 1988. (An awareness scrapbook/journal for kids living in two separate families.)

Ford, Melanie, Steven Ford, Annie Ford, and Jann Blackstone-Ford. *My Parents Are Divorced Too*. Washington, DC: Magination Press, 2006. (Three stepsiblings in a blended family discuss their experiences, and those of friends, with divorce and remarriage. These young authors write about their own experiences frankly and clearly, in a way that can be understood by young readers. More than just a recounting of experiences, it is a guidebook for getting adjusted to a new life, and a means for opening new avenues of communication at a difficult time in everyone's life. Ages eight to twelve.)

Goldman, Katie. *In the Wings*. New York: Dial, 1982.

Holyoke, Nancy, and Scott Nash. *Help!: A Girl's Guide to Divorce and Stepfamilies*. Middleton, Wisconsin: Pleasant Company Publications, 1999.

Klein, Norma. *Breaking Up: A Novel*. New York: Alfred A. Knopf, 1980.

Krementz, Jill. *How It Feels When Parents Divorce*. New York: Alfred A. Knopf, 1988. (A sensitive view of the experiences of children, mostly adolescents, who were interviewed and photographed.)

Schab, Lisa. *The Divorce Workbook for Teens: Activities to Help You Move Beyond the Breakup*. Oakland, California: New Harbinger Publications, 2008.

Voigt, Cynthia. *A Solitary Blue*. New York: Atheneum Books, 2012. (A sophisticated, sensitive story about a high school boy, Jeff, who resolves his feelings about his custodial father and absent mother. Jeff's mother, who deserted the family years before, re-enters his life and challenges Jeff to overcome his pain about his family.)

MOVIES AND TV

Split is a powerful movie that features a number of children, aged six to twelve, talking about the effects of their parents' divorces. Whether you watch it with your children or not, you will be moved and it will help you support your children's experience: *www.splitfilm.org*.

There are many movies and books that can stimulate discussions with your children about divorce. I recommend that you preview them before sharing them with your children, as some may not be age-appropriate. You can find lists of them here: *www.commonsensemedia.org/lists/movies-to-help-kids-understand-divorce*.

Index

About the Author

ANN GOLD BUSCHO, PHD, is a licensed clinical psychologist who specializes in family issues and issues related to divorce, parenting, parenting planning, and co-parenting counseling. She has professional and personal experience in nesting, co-parenting, stepparenting, and single-parenting issues. She has presented widely at state and national conferences for attorneys, mental health professionals, and financial professionals on collaborative divorce, forgiveness practices, nesting during divorce, and consensual dispute resolution.

Dr. Buscho is also a cofounder of a residential treatment program for traumatized emergency responders and their families at which she volunteers regularly. A graduate of Stanford University and the California Graduate School of Psychology, she lives in San Rafael, California.

She writes regularly for *Psychology Today* (www.psychologytoday .com/us/blog/better-divorce?eml) and other online publications, and has been a frequent guest on podcasts and radio programs relating to family issues. This is her first book.